THE MURDER

—— *of* ——

DOROTHY MILLIKEN

Cold Case in Maine

Sharon Kitchens

THE
History
PRESS

Published by The History Press
An imprint of Arcadia Publishing
Charleston, SC
www.historypress.com

Front cover, clockwise from top left: Dorothy on her wedding day, 1973. *Courtesy of the Rancourt family*; Early morning photo of Dorothy's car parked in front of the Beal's Laundromat. *Courtesy of the Sun Journal*; Dorothy at age seventeen. *Courtesy of the Rancourt family*; Scene of the crime at Beal's Laundromat in Lewiston on November 6, 1976. *Courtesy of the Sun Journal; photo by Simokaitis*.

Back cover: Lewiston Police Department's Criminal Investigation Office as it looked in 1985 when on the first floor of city hall. Detectives on Dorothy's case would have worked out of this room. *Courtesy of Dave Gudas*.

First published 2025

Manufactured in the United States

ISBN 9781467159449

Library of Congress Control Number: 2025933736

For Dorothy

CONTENTS

ACKNOWLEDGEMENTS

Faulkner and Tennessee, my lovable shadows, you keep momma on her toes.

Anne Marie and Roland for your savvy and encouragement and all those incredible meals at the North Pole.

Michelle for all the books and being the best road trip buddy.

Hannah for all the words and the deftly handled red pen. You can have all the Reese's. There would be no books without you.

Meredith and Olive for all the forest walks.

Kristen Seavey, creator of the podcast *Murder, She Told*, for the ethics lessons.

Judith Meyer, executive editor *Sun Journal*, for your wisdom.

For your expertise and invaluable insights, Lyndon Abbott and Dr. Margaret Greenwald, you were each tremendous. Thank you for helping me get the details right. Any and all errors are my own.

Bruce Robert Coffin and Don Goulet, a couple of the good ones. Joseph L. Giacalone, retired NYPD sergeant. Mike Parks for the auto stuff. Mark Nickerson, president of the Maine State Troopers, for the stories.

The Lewiston and Portland Public Libraries. I left with my mind and arms full every trip. Thank you for absolutely every single thing you magical librarians do everywhere every day—you are my heroes.

Members of the Sabattus Historical Society for the history.

Thank you to Dorothy's family and friends for trusting me with this story. Mary Ellen and Bob for the hours you each spent in person and over the phone traveling back in time. The shared love you have of your sister burns an eternal flame. George, your keen observations and gentle nudges to key people opened doors. Peggy for all the calls, texts, hosting, wrangling, cheerleading. Glenda, Sue, Diana and Sheila for all the memories.

I'm indebted to Tonia Ross for supporting my journey and ensuring the narrative of her mother is accurate and for helping open channels of communication with people who knew Dorothy best. She bravely answered every question I had. I remain in awe of her courage.

And great thanks to The History Press dream team of Mike, Maddison and Dani.

AUTHOR'S NOTE

When my editor asked me if I would consider writing a true crime book, I told him absolutely not. Yet the next morning I found myself settling into my favorite reading chair and pulling up the Maine State Police's Unsolved Homicides webpage. A few clicks later, and I was reading about Dorothy Milliken, who was found lying outside a laundromat in Lewiston at 4:45 a.m. on November 6, 1976. How she had left the home she shared with her husband approximately six hours earlier and frequently did her laundry late at night or early in the morning.

And all at once I was drawn in, scribbling literally line after line of questions in my spiral-bound notebook. Following this exercise, in short order I phoned a couple of friends who are former detectives and asked them what they thought. Should I do this? They said yes, you can help bring attention to the case. One even offered to put me in touch with a sergeant with the Maine State Police. So, I pursued it, first meeting with the detective in charge of the investigation and then with a representative for the family. At both meetings, I said, "I'll walk away if you want." I wasn't so naïve as to think I could solve this thing or bring closure, but I would listen and go down a deep rabbit hole to tell this young woman's story. Because to me she is the story just as much as what happened to her.

In all my interactions with Dorothy's friends and members of her family, I tried to be responsible. Was I always? I don't know. Every meeting I set up, every call or text I made, I was asking people to relive what may be the worst day of their life. It was a constant balance trying to be kind but also needing to get the details right—because believe me every single detail from the color of a shirt to whether a high school trip lasted a week or ten days to the brand of cigarettes smoked—it all matters a lot. When those details are all loved ones have left and they've been wrong in the press, that grates, that hurts.

True crime can retraumatize people. My hope is that with this book, in addition to telling Dorothy's story, maybe fans of true crime can see how it can be done ethically. With the consent and participation of family. With the understanding that these are real people and what happened to them decades ago still traumatizes them today.

Though I had total access to family members and friends, there were some serious limitations to my reporting efforts. The window of opportunity to talk to a number of the people who were part of the initial investigation had closed when I began my research. However, I have been able to track down a remarkable number of credible sources who indulged my curiosity and generously allowed me to dredge up the past. Overall, I interviewed nearly four dozen people.

When it came to understanding the anatomy of a homicide investigation, at times this one specifically, the insight and patience of current and former law enforcement, forensic specialists and subject-matter experts were key to helping me reconstruct the subsequent investigation and navigate the complexities, exposing why it went cold.

I drew much of the historical context from visits to the Lewiston Public Library and conversations with members of the Sabattus Historical Society. I also relied on old newspaper articles, archival documents and books by a variety of subject experts.

I did not have access to the several inch-thick blue binders kept by the state police documenting the case. These would theoretically contain forensic reports, witness lists and statements, a victimology report, photos and sketches of the crime scene, officer at scene reports and more. Those remain on a shelf at the state trooper barracks in Gray.

I filed several Freedom of Information Act requests for investigative reports for open and closed cases from the 1970s that shared some of the characteristics of Dorothy's case. All were rejected. In Maine, the state's policy is to deny all requests for investigative records created before 1995.

FROM ASSISTANT ATTORNEY GENERAL Jonathan Bolton on June 11, 2024:

> *I have been authorized to provide the following response to your inquires:*
> *The Office of Attorney General and the Unsolved Homicide Unit work*
> *directly with family members regarding access to information concerning*
> *both open and closed investigations. Pursuant to statute, there is no general*
> *public access to investigative files from before 1995.*

A follow-up response from Bolton in response to my request for the chapter and section in existing state law that blocks access to investigative files pre-1995:

> *The provision is Section 11 of chapter 719 of the Public Laws of 1993.*

The relevant section of the legislation essentially dictates that documents should not be released to the public if they interfere with law enforcement proceedings, constitute an unwarranted invasion of personal privacy and disclose investigative techniques and procedures, among other things.

Trying to gain access to a court transcript proved to be an obstacle course. An expert on Maine cold cases not employed by the state told me it's an "obnoxious process" that involves "jumping through hoops." It certainly is and did. The Maine State Law and Legislative Reference Library directed me to the Androscoggin Superior Court, where a clerk told me records did not exist prior to the mid-1980s. A follow-up call to the library involved a wonderful person who told me it's not unusual for clerks to lie or be misinformed and then gave me the docket number for the case I was querying, advising me to go back to the court. I did, at which point I was made aware of a form that needed completing before a request could be made. When I clarified that I was primarily interested in the transcript I was advised to contact the Office of Transcript Operations. There, an individual told me without me filling out another form and submitting a request it would not be possible to tell me if a transcript exists and that furthermore older transcripts were limited because stenographers who have since passed kept the transcripts.

Ultimately, I felt my time could be better spent knocking on doors and proceeded without the desired transcript. I'm being transparent with you, dear reader, should you decide to seek information from the State of Maine about a cold case prior to 1995 so you know what you're up against.

About This Book

I refer to certain family members and friends by first name only for their privacy. I refer to Dorothy throughout, feeling it inappropriate to call her Dotty, the nickname she adopted with family and friends.

I use the terms *cold case* and *unsolved homicide* interchangeably. There is no uniform definition of *cold case homicide* nationally. In the state of Maine, an unsolved homicide is described as a known or potential homicide case in which three years or more have passed without anyone being charged.

The book's sections are organized similar to an investigation. I chose to begin and conclude with the victims' stories because in the end, they matter the most. First Dorothy and then her family and friends. Woven through the narrative are information about and insights into how active investigations and cold cases are worked in Maine and crime scene forensics.

Tips and information about Dorothy Milliken and/or any unsolved or missing persons case in Maine can be submitted to the Maine State Police:

1-800-228-0857 (207-624-7076)
https://www.maine.gov/dps/msp/about/report-crime/major-crimes-unit-central

A PERCENTAGE OF PROCEEDS from this book are being donated to the Forensic Anthropology Identification and Recovery (FAIR) Lab at the University of New Hampshire. The FAIR Lab trains students to excavate, recover and identify human remains in northern New England.

LIST OF CHARACTERS

Family

Dorothy "Dotty" (maiden name Rancourt) Milliken

George Walter Rancourt, also known as Pépère (married to Dorothy St. Onge)—referred to as George W.

George Ronaldo Rancourt—Dorothy's father—referred to as Ronaldo

Lois Ellen Prince—Dorothy's mother

Bob—Dorothy's older brother

Mary Ellen—Dorothy's older sister

Peggy—Dorothy's younger sister

Moe—Peggy's husband

George Ronaldo Rancourt Jr.—Dorothy's younger brother—referred to as George Jr.

Tonia Ross—Dorothy and Gerald's older daughter

Erica—Dorothy and Peter's younger daughter

Little Pete—Dorothy and Peter's son

Gerald Arsenault—Dorothy's ex-husband and Tonia's father

Peter Milliken—Dorothy's second husband, Erica and Little Pete's father

Friends

Gail Ann—neighbor living in Dorothy's house at the time of her death
Diana—high school friend of Dorothy's
Glenda—high school friend of Dorothy's
Sheila—high school friend of Dorothy's
Sue—high school friend of Dorothy's
Glenys—married to Peter before Dorothy

Authorities

Lyndon Abbott—detective, Maine State Police (MSP) (1964–1985)
Roger Bisson—sergeant, Lewiston Police Department (LPD) (1962–1987)
Michael Chavez—detective corporal, MSP Unsolved Homicide Unit, has had Dorothy's case since 2012
Richard S. Cohen—assistant attorney general (served as attorney general from 1978 to 1981)
Lionel Cote—Androscoggin County sheriff (January 1976–June 1980) and police chief Town of Sabattus (June 1974–December 1976)
Thomas Delahanty II—district attorney Prosecutorial District 3 for Androscoggin, Franklin and Oxford Counties (1975–1980)
Larry Gilbert—LPD (1969–1994—he retired as chief of police), mayor of Lewiston (2007–2012)
Kenneth Gilman—patrol, LPD (1973–1984)
Thomas Goodwin—assistant attorney general during the 1990s
Lucien Longtin—LPD chief of police (1968–1980), was with LPD by 1957
Peter McCarthy—investigator, MSP (1969–1993)
Willard Parker—detective, MSP (1957–1977)
Thomas Pickering—lieutenant, MSP (commanding officer of Unsolved Homicide Unit since 2023)
James Pinette—detective, MSP (1964–1984)
Bruce Rafnell—detective, MSP (1970–1990), had Dorothy's case from mid-November 1976 to the early 1990s
Dr. Henry Ryan—chief medical examiner for State of Maine (1976–1998)
Robert Soucy—detective captain, LPD (1956–retired from the force in 1979 as captain of detectives)

AN ACCOUNTING

It was a Friday, five days after Halloween in 1976. Carved pumpkins still sat on porches, the flesh on the bottoms mushy. Bowls had been emptied of chocolate bars and candy corn. Plastic skeletons and paper decorations in the shape of cats and witches were stored away.

The spookiest time of the year was supposedly done, but on that unusually warm late fall day, a light, haunting wind swept through Western Maine.

In the quiet rural town of Sabattus, it was just another day for most residents—bustling kids off to school, dropping in on neighbors, going to hair appointments, working a factory shift in a nearby town. The Steve Miller Band's "Rock'n Me" played on the radio. Plans were made to see John Carpenter's film *Assault on Precinct 13*.

Twenty-seven-year-old Dorothy Milliken, a mother of three, was drinking copious amounts of coffee and stressing out about money and her sick baby. She felt weighed down, in over her head. Dorothy was due back at work as an assistant in a local dentist's office in a few days. On Monday, her two-and-a-half-month-old son was going in for surgery. And she had a substantial amount of laundry to do and no washing machine or dryer in the house. None of these concerns would matter anymore in a number of hours because she would be killed.

In the 1970s, violent crime was very unusual in Maine. Murders were infrequent and remembered forever. Citizens didn't usually lock their cars or even their homes. Sabattus in particular offered an idyllic place to be a child. Kids ran through fields, skated on or swam in local ponds depending on the season and bought ice cream and sodas from shop owners who knew them and their parents. There was a dark side, but that was mostly inside homes hidden away from public view.

When Dorothy was growing up, she and her older sister, Mary Ellen, shared a bedroom on the second floor of an old farmhouse heated by a wood-fired stove in the kitchen. During the long Maine winters, it was their nighttime routine to put a brick in the oven, heat it up and wrap it in a towel. "One, two, three, up the stairs we'd go and jump in our beds," says Mary Ellen. "The cool air felt good, and once under the heavy down-filled covers it was really nice."

It was her childhood home Dorothy departed sometime after 11:00 p.m. to drive to a twenty-four-hour-laundromat in the neighboring old mill town of Lewiston to do her laundry. From that point on, no one knows for certain Dorothy's movements.

Beginning in the late 1950s, the gargantuan textile mills in downtown Lewiston started to empty out, and by the mid-1970s, they had become an inescapable reminder of the town's economic misfortunes. Many of the retail businesses that had benefited from them were closing up or closed. The industrial spirit still lingered, but the downtown was notorious as a place of in-your-face grittiness where the booze flowed and drugs were exchanged. Authorities were said to be known to overlook certain illegal activities.

The laundromat was located on Lisbon Street, otherwise known as ME-196, a main thoroughfare bisecting Lewiston and connecting it with nearby communities. As it was located in a thicket of well-kept homes and three-story apartment buildings in a quieter part of town known more for its commercial businesses, there was not much walking traffic.

Dorothy frequented the place weekly. She sometimes went at night with her mother but more often during the day with one of her sisters or her daughter Tonia. The then four-year-old loved spending time with her mom and helping her load the washing machines lined up along the wall. Tonia would eat popcorn out of a paper bag from the laundromat's little machine and push the metal carts around. She still remembers being fascinated by the dry-cleaning conveyor belt and delighted by Anne Laplante, the kind attendant with the little office in the front corner. Barely able to reach the tables in the middle of the room where Dorothy folded her clothes, Tonia sat in one of the plastic chairs with her coloring books and crayons.

Tonia can only ever recall them parking by the side entrance on Dumont Avenue. They'd bring their bundles of laundry in, passing the brown-colored bathroom in the back corner. On the evening of November 5, however, Dorothy parked in front of the well-lit laundromat, choosing—it's believed—to be more visible.

Approximately three hours later, having washed and dried her clothes, Dorothy was in the process of folding them when someone drew her into the open air—a monster emerging from and then disappearing into the darkness. His face close and cold as he pummeled her and she screamed into the dark and silent night.

Her body slumped against the outside wall. A blue dome light eventually punctuating the predawn dark. Dorothy Milliken became a name typed on an index card filed at state police headquarters in Augusta. Her crime scene displayed in grainy black-and-white photos in the evening newspapers.

No murder weapon has surfaced, no motive realized, no arrests ever made, yet investigators say they have a "deluge of information" and five people they—as of 2021—could not rule out. Nearly five decades later, the murder remains one of Maine's most notorious cold cases. Everyone has a theory. It's the husband, it's one of the tough guys he hung out with, it was organized crime, a serial killer, a rogue cop and on and on. People who know things are reluctant to talk, keeping their bad secrets.

What, though, if we're not talking about a Hannibal Lecter? It was brutal and an act of madness, clearly. But what are the chances this was just some ordinary man? Probably not even that smart, but because he has not been identified he is shrouded in mystery. What if Dorothy was just in the wrong place at the wrong time?

And then there's this: that weekend, in a town where a violent murder was rare, there was a second similar homicide. At the local fairgrounds, a stable hand by the name of Robert McBride was beaten to death around the same time Dorothy was killed. A twenty-year-old suspect was quickly identified, scooped up, tried, convicted, sentenced to life in prison and released eight years later. Police have publicly dismissed a connection and remain tight-lipped about both investigations.

1

FOREVER YOUNG

THE GIRL

A blue-eyed beauty with a thousand-watt smile, heavy black hair and porcelain skin, Dorothy Rancourt was one of the prettiest girls for miles.

Everyone who knew her called her Dotty, a name she adopted after learning a close friend's sister also named Dorothy abbreviated her name that way. She enjoyed making people laugh, whether by blowing smoke rings or faking a British accent. A tiny woman at 5'1", Dorothy might have weighed around 110 pounds soaking wet, but she was not easily intimidated. She would tell anyone where the bear crapped in the woods.

A giver not a taker, easygoing, uncomplaining. By high school, she'd become a fan of the alternative universes and extraterrestrial life in monster movies and the CBS science fiction television series *Lost in Space*. As a teenage girl in the 1960s, she swooned over Elvis Presley and the Beatles—especially drummer Ringo Starr. She'd twirl her hair when she was tired. Dorothy didn't gossip—if she had something to say, she'd say it straight. She enjoyed collecting rocks everywhere but especially at Popham Beach in Phippsburg. As Dorothy grew into womanhood, she became attentive to her clothes and was known for her up-to-date looks cultivated from thrift shops and department stores. She took tremendous satisfaction in cleaning her home.

Dorothy was a champion coffee consumer. She would drink a pot of coffee cold all day long. Black. No sugar, no cream. Another thing about her, she loved to eat. Dorothy would eat an onion like it was an apple. She liked spaghetti, chop suey and her mom's brown bread. When she had eggs, she drowned them in Heinz ketchup. In her senior high school memory book, she wrote she loved "just about any food that can be eaten."

More than anything, she derived pleasure from being a mother. Dorothy sang the children's Bible song "It's Bubbling in My Soul" to her kids. She picked flowers with her eldest daughter, Tonia, soothed her, painted her nails, made her hot cocoa on cold days and spoke to her as an adult—but always gently.

Dorothy could be attracted to danger—to bad boys. She enjoyed attention. She could be reactive and make poor choices because she was a human being. Dorothy didn't have a romanticized image of life because she couldn't afford one. At twenty-seven, she knew what she was up against. It may have been the clearest view of her circumstances she'd ever had. Her life was idling, and there were big decisions that had to be made. If Dorothy had been given the opportunity to figure things out, who knows what she could have done.

HOMETOWN

The middle child of six children of Franco-American parents, Dorothy was born on Tuesday, July 5, 1949, in Lila Lidbeck's Maternity House in Lisbon, Maine. She grew up in the small dirt road town of Sabattus. The borough is surrounded by five communities: the former industrial hub of Lewiston; Lisbon, which is known as the birthplace of the soda Moxie and as Stephen King's childhood home; the liberal college town of Bowdoin; and the small towns of Wales and Greene.

Historically, most travelers who visit Maine seek out the ocean views of the DownEast coast and MidCoast. These regions and the millions of vacationers attracted to them are the inspiration for the state's slogan "Vacationland," which first appeared on Maine car license plates in 1936. The part of Maine where Dorothy and her family come from has long identified with having more acres of land than people and is mostly bypassed by visitors. Towns where, as one creeps a block or two beyond main streets back into wooded areas, people can be found eking out a daily existence.

Sabattus is just under twenty-seven square miles and in 1960 had a population of fewer than 1,300. During Dorothy's childhood, it was a quiet rural community. People farmed and worked in the same mills their grandparents had.

In recent years, the area has changed as developers have sought to remake the landscape and provide housing to the area's increasing population. To people who grew up in Sabattus in particular, their town has become something almost unrecognizable. Dirt roads have been paved. Trailers and quickly erected ramshackle homes now line once bucolic country roads. More commuters and far fewer farmers.

"There were twenty-two dairy farms in town," Mike Deslauriers, president of the Sabattus Historical Society, says. "You couldn't go anywhere that you didn't see cows. Now we have none. There are no more dairy farms."

Tidy two-story brick houses like the one Dorothy was raised in, surrounded by vegetable gardens and fields, are as uncommon today as the small ponds where she and her siblings waded during the summer months. To hunt and fish, people have to travel farther. A gaggle of kids pedaling their bicycles down a road in Sabattus would no longer be seen as a good idea. Too many fast cars.

Sabattus was incorporated in 1840 as part of the larger town of Webster. The village was settled in 1774 by Robert Ross, a man from the nearby town of Brunswick who sought to lay down roots. His arrival was followed by industrialists such as Robert Niles, who built a number of saw- and gristmills that were powered from the Sabattus River. By the early 1980s, they'd been torn down.

Those mills, like the much larger ones in nearby Lewiston and its sister city Auburn, attracted people of French heritage from the Canadian cities of Quebec and New Brunswick—so much so that the community of Franco-American families was targeted by the hate group the Ku Klux Klan in the early 1900s. Crosses burned on lawns for a time. This and a shared heritage only drew the Franco-American community tighter.

Up until the 1970s, if you lived in Lewiston or one of the surrounding communities, it would have been common to hear people speaking French. As time progressed, school-age children and their older siblings spoke primarily English, which was taught in area schools, and many homes became bilingual. Dorothy and her siblings did not speak French; their father and paternal grandfather did.

The Farm

Dorothy's childhood home was a modest nineteenth-century farmhouse with low-ceilinged rooms and hardwood floors that connected to a large barn. The kitchen was anchored by a wood stove, which was expected to heat the house along with a wood furnace in the basement. For Dorothy and her siblings, it was a place they could be wild and free. The house, one of few, was located on the Williams Road several miles from the town center and school. You might see one or two cars a day. The front door opened up to three hundred acres of green fields.

Growing up, Dorothy and her older sister, Mary Ellen, were ravenous for the outdoors. They lived for adventures. Fishing and swimming in the local brook. The first ones in the cold April water. Always climbing.

"Dotty and I were tree climbers," Mary Ellen laughingly recalls. "Dotty got in a tree and that tree went right over, but didn't break. And we loved the barn. We'd climb on the beams and everything. Dad did not like it all. We made sure we did it when he was not around."

They would lie on the backs of a pair of steers and brush them, though only when their father wasn't around, Mary Ellen admits. The family's horses were paid equal attention. "We'd go down to the fence and we'd make sure we had apples," Mary Ellen says. "We'd jump on the horses' backs and take off through the woods and go right up through the pasture."

When they were six and eight, Dorothy and Mary Ellen decided to go to Portland to buy some lipstick. "Towards evening we went down the road, and my dad was on the side of the road all the way down and made noises and scared the living crap out of us and we ran back home," shares Mary Ellen. "We thought a moose was out there. Daddy wouldn't let us wear lipstick, and we wanted to."

Dorothy's younger sister, Peggy, recalls how stubborn Dorothy could be when she was an adolescent. "Every morning my father would be cooking and my sister would come downstairs," Peggy says. "She wasn't happy about getting up in the morning. My father would say, 'Good morning,' and then he would go up to her and he would hug her and say, 'I love you, tell me you love me,' and she would not. He would say, 'I'm going to squeeze you until you say you love me,' and she was so stubborn. 'No, Daddy I'm not going to tell you,' she'd say. It was so funny. He was a teaser. She loved him so much, but she was so stubborn."

On Saturday nights, the family would drink Kool-Aid—which the kids called "Bug Juice"—and eat popcorn and watch the popular *Lawrence Welk Show* on television. On Sundays they'd attend services at West Bowdoin Baptist Church, where Lois's family were longtime members and had a pew.

FAMILY

Pépère

George W. Rancourt, known as Pépère—pronounced "pay pehr" and meaning *grandpa*—to his grandchildren, was a storied member of the Rancourt clan. "He was an old person meaning from yester school," an acquaintance shares. "He didn't look at things anything like they do now."

George W. was born into a farming family on Sunday, April 3, 1892, in Hallowell, Maine. As a teenager, he began working in the brickyards in Lewiston. It has been said he could shovel the wet clay they made bricks with till it would put most men right under. His fellow workers could not keep up with him. It was this hard labor that broke his body in later years. Dorothy's eldest daughter, Tonia, describes him as bowlegged and hunchbacked.

On November 10, 1913, he married Dorothy St. Onge. He was twenty-two; she was eighteen and worked in a local shoe factory. Their marriage was a happy one. In August 1916, they had George Ronaldo, followed through the years by three girls and a boy. Then, in 1941, while they were living in a little house on Pleasant Ridge Road, tragedy struck. Dorothy was holding onto a brass bed frame by an open window during a thunderstorm. Lightning hit the bed, and she was electrocuted. This was the same bedroom where her great-granddaughter Tonia would live for a short while thirty-five years later.

George W. was at work, and it was their twenty-five-year-old son, Ronaldo, who picked his mother up, took her outside and laid her down on the porch to try to revive her.

During his later years, George W. moved in with Ronaldo and his family. He fawned over the grandchildren and great-grandchildren, giving them candy from his pockets and making jokes. Tonia remembers him telling her to step in the fresh cow patties because it would make her grow, so she'd step in cow patties in her bare feet thinking, *I'm going to grow*.

The adults in his life knew him for the little glasses of homemade hard cider and elderberry wine he made in and carried up from the basement.

Another of his exploits for which he has a lasting reputation are the illegal cock fights he organized out in the field behind his home every spring and early summer. A neighbor who chose to remain anonymous described knowing without even looking out the window at the road every car that went down the road in front of their house by the sound of the rattle it made going over the ripples. They said there were "all kinds of fancy Cadillacs and a lot of drinking."

Daddy *"The Gentle Giant"*

A handsome man in a salt-of-the-earth way, George Ronaldo Rancourt stood around 5'5" tall. Dorothy's younger sister, Peggy, mainly remembers him with lots of silver hair.

Friends and associates called him by his middle name, "Ronaldo," when he was growing up. He hated the name because he said it sounded like a "damn old Tomcat."

In his teens and early twenties, he boxed under the name Tiger Jack. His most famous opponent was featherweight boxer Maurice "Lefty" Lachance, who would go on to fight four world champions.

Around the time Ronaldo lost to Lachance, he enlisted in the U.S. Navy, serving from March 13, 1942, to October 2, 1945. He served as a motor machinist's mate third class on the USS *George E. Badger*, a Clemson-class destroyer named after the secretary of the navy in 1841. Ronaldo helped operate, maintain and repair equipment aboard the ship. On June 5, 1945, the destroyer encountered a tropical storm with winds close to ninety miles per hour near Okinawa. He helped pump five or six feet of water out of a steering engine room and secure the hatches. It was a day to remember for the crew.

Aside from a brief stint working in a textile mill, for most of his life, Ronaldo worked doing wooding and farming and had an awful time trying to get ahead. Still, he always made time to help out neighbors—whether dropping off a glass jug of milk or shoeing oxen free of charge. "If a neighbor didn't have much, Daddy would quietly help however he could," says Peggy.

Dorothy paid close attention to how her father interacted with others and was his little shadow when running errands. For the weekly shop they'd go to Huen's Market, the town's main grocer, located on the corner of Main Street in the tiny downtown. William Huen had owned the store since 1912 and worked as a clerk for a dozen years prior when it was called Bangs Grocery Store. Wooden barrels of crackers and big dill pickles greeted shoppers as they entered. A customer who needed a roast would be taken into the cooler to pick the side from the animal hanging in the freezer.

Huen let several regulars, including Ronaldo, add charges to an account all winter and had them settle up in the spring. This was known locally as "keeping it on the slip." Several members of the Sabattus Historical Society say he assisted a lot of people, that Huen helped carry the town.

Sometime in the 1950s, when Dorothy was still a little girl, Huen retired and turned the shop over to his nephew. Presumably by that time, both her father and Huen's paying it forward had left a strong impression on her. As an adult, she was generous with people who needed help.

Peggy remembers her father's hands as being tanned and rough from the hard work he did, but gentle. She recalls feeling a sense of security in those big hands when he would stroke her hair.

According to Peggy, the family's barn cats would jump on his shoulders. If he was working in the woods during hunting season and saw a deer, he would stand still and watch it. If hunters happened upon him and asked if he'd seen any deer, he would say no. He told her the deer were so pretty he didn't want to see them get killed.

Mama

Ronaldo had always liked Lois, a hardworking and timid girl he knew from next door. Once he was home from the war, they enjoyed a brief courtship before marrying in June 1946 at West Bowdoin Baptist Church.

Lois Ellen Prince was born on March 17, 1918, and grew up in the Sabattus area. Her father, Arlon, was a farmer who, like his few neighbors, sold whatever he could grow, raise or make—mainly butter, eggs, berries, vegetables, pork, beef and wood. His ancestor William Brewster (c. 1566–1644) was one of the 102 passengers and 30 or so crew who set sail from England for what became Plymouth, Massachusetts, on the *Mayflower* on September 16, 1620.

Her mother, Amanda (Jordan), sold dahlias she grew in a flower garden on the little farm. Lois would inherit her lifelong passion for gardening. In her spare time, Amanda painted outdoor scenes.

When Lois was growing up, there was no bus to take her to high school in town. So, when she was fourteen years old, her parents sent her to a home four miles closer to town where she would live while attending school. The house was owned by Myrtie and Edwin, a fairly well-off childless couple who took in single people and rural children for extra money. Some of the kids would work off their room and board by helping out. Myrtie was a good friend of Amanda's, so this might have made the situation feel more agreeable.

Edwin, who was in his late fifties at the time, seduced Lois and she became pregnant. Her family took her back in for several months, and she gave birth to a little boy in 1934. Unaware of who the father was, Lois's parents agreed to let the couple adopt the newborn and sent her back to live with them as a boarder again. Lois must have been traumatized by this experience, having been sexually assaulted and being forced to live in the house with a fifty-eight-year-old predator and infant son.

Two years later, Lois became pregnant again by Edwin. This time her parents kept her and her newborn son, Bob, at home. When Lois's dad, Arlon, found out years later, it was all Lois's sisters could do to stop him from trying to shoot Edwin. One took the rifle and hid it.

In her later years, Lois spoke to Mary Ellen about how she thought Edwin had loved her. Peggy believes her mother was flattered by his attention and the money.

For a long time, even after she was married, Lois felt judged by people in the community, but she stood steady, carrying the trauma from her younger years silently uncomplaining. Her life was rooted in the family she raised and her church group. But she taught her children, "If you don't have something nice to say about a person don't say anything at all." Dorothy learned about keeping pain to herself and rarely opened up to family and even rarer still to friends.

Bob

Bob was around ten years old when Lois married Ronaldo, who tried to adopt him. Amanda put a kibosh to that, and Bob continued to live with and be raised by her until his junior year in high school. Feeling like no one wanted him, he began acting out. Mostly getting into fights, but on at least one occasion, he broke a neon sign on the town's main street with a rock sling. After that incident, Ronaldo brought Bob to live with him and Lois. Bob has always considered Ronaldo his real father and says if it wasn't for him, he'd have ended up in prison. Instead, he went into the Marine Corps.

Expanding Family

In 1947, Lois and George had Mary Ellen, followed two years later by Dorothy and, two years after that, Peggy. George was born in 1956. Lois gave up work in the mills to be a stay-at-home mom while the kids were young.

Remember the Brown Bread

Lois was a wonderful cook who enjoyed bringing her family together at the table and feeding them. Her children rave to this day about her spaghetti and meatballs, the thick rich gravy she made with drippings from roast beef and her plain-flavored donuts.

Every Saturday she made a pot of baked beans with homegrown beans and onions and a hunk of pork from a pig on the farm. Sometimes she made an extra pot for the church if they were having a fundraising dinner. "We grow our own farts," Ronaldo would say.

Accompanying beans was her famous brown bread, which was baked in a repurposed peanut butter tin. When it came out of the oven, Ronaldo would take a string and cut thick slices of the bread.

BEST FRIENDS

At Sabattus High School, there was no cafeteria, so kids who lived nearby walked home for lunch or brought their own. There was also no gym. When Dorothy and her teammates practiced basketball, they played on the second floor of the Sabattus Town Hall. Only a year or two before she started attending, the six-room two-story school, built in 1898, got indoor plumbing. On windy days, the windows shook. There were rats in the cellar.

School life continued pretty much the same way it had up to that point. Dorothy arrived in a skirt and blouse as was expected of girls at the time, carrying a nickel for a bottle of milk and a green lunchbox containing a wax paper–wrapped sandwich. She went to school with the same kids. There were forty in Dorothy's class, eighty-eight total in the school. The joke was you couldn't get a pencil without everybody knowing about it.

The first day of freshman year, the teacher told the roomful of students, "Half of your grade will leave school." Sure enough, only twenty graduated. Kids could quit at fifteen, and some did to work on the family farm. This was a small agricultural town, and the kids knew what was expected of them. No one challenged it. The school didn't have a guidance counselor, though some teachers took on that role when needed, and college representatives didn't come calling. Later on, boys volunteered to fight in Vietnam, heading to Saigon and places like Phuoc Tuy Province.

Dorothy threw her heart and soul into her high school experience as much as she could. She was one of a group of girls who met on the playground when they were about five years old. Dorothy, Glenda, Sheila and Sue became five only four years later when Diana moved into a house up the street from Sue. Diana's grandmother and Sue's grandmother were sisters.

High School Daze

No one's family had a lot of money, so options were limited, but by high school, they were a pack of girls bounding from one adventure to another in a buttoned-up small town. Diana, Glenda, Sheila and Sue continued to walk to school together and occasionally hang out at Sheila or Sue's. On weekends, whoever was available would bike out to Dorothy's.

Dorothy and her friends were emblematic of small-town kids in the 1960s who weren't raised with a lot of money or parental supervision but who, like all kids everywhere, had fun at times and struggled at times. While some dreamed of leaving, others only knew they wanted to stay. As children, they saw Sabattus and Lisbon and the high school gymnasiums where they played or attended basketball games, and that was pretty much it, with limited exceptions. They didn't meet strangers, but talking to them in 2024, they also didn't feel where they grew up was claustrophobic. It was what it was, real.

DIANA WAS EASYGOING, THE life of the party. The class clown. She also had brains and interests that expanded beyond the county line. Her achievements included basketball, cheerleading and class government. She was involved in the Scarlet Cadets, a marching band in the Lewiston-Auburn area that competed around New England in stadiums and parades.

When Diana was thirteen, her baby brother was born, so she ended up watching him after school and making dinner because her mom worked nights.

Her junior and senior years, she worked three jobs on weekends, including at Kentucky Fried Chicken and the Lewiston Drive-In, saving money for college because her parents couldn't afford tuition. Diana also applied for scholarships and grants and wrote essays for prize money. All her hard work paid off, and she went far—graduating from the University of Maine in Farmington, teaching and even living in Europe.

Diana visited Dorothy and Mary Ellen during the summers.

Glenda was the straight talker, always up for anything. The girl who laughed the loudest and always had your back. A tough exterior but a gentle soul. She and Dorothy smoked cigarettes in the girls' bathroom in the basement.

Her parents split up when she was fifteen, which left her cooking and cleaning. She got a car when she graduated and made the payments herself. "My father was not anyone you'd bring your friends home to meet," she shares. "I remember staying at Sheila's house once. Her parents were much more receptive to her having friends over. My father was drunk a lot after my mother left. I had more freedom but still not a lot. My dad knew Dotty's dad, so it was OK if she came over before games. He wasn't there anyways. Alice Labonte (another classmate) had the car. We'd chip in for gas. A quarter bought a gallon of gas back then."

Glenda has fond memories of Eddie Jillson, a young family man who was the custodian and bus driver for the Sabattus schools. For a time, he also coached the girls' basketball team. Among the happy memories Glenda has of school was being at Jillson's house and painting a big scoreboard to put in front of the high school. Thinking of Jillson, she says she never rode the bus except once when it was twenty below one morning and he stopped the bus and gave her a ride to school. She had a mini dress on and had about frozen her legs off.

Sheila was outgoing and the organizer and mother of the group. She knew the facts of life and told the girls about menstruation. Sheila and Diana led the class fundraising projects together. There were fundraisers for athletic uniforms, the senior year class trip, everything.

After high school, Sheila went to Waterville for training at a lab tech school.

Sue had rheumatic fever as a child so her mother never wanted her to exert herself in sports, so she enjoyed cheering on her friends. Her mother was the only stay-at-home mom in the group. Occasionally, the girls would hang out at her house. Sue remains a great storyteller and the de facto historian of the group.

Hoops and Cheers

Because Dorothy lived a car ride's distance from her friends and school, the only semi-daily activity she shared with them in high school was basketball.

On the basketball court, she was a scrapper. Like Diana and Glenda, she'd fight for the ball. They were tough, and when they came together, they won most of their games. The girls would enjoy a post-game dinner with teammates at the McDonald's in Lewiston because that's where you could get change back.

Diana, Glenda and, during their senior year, Sheila were also cheerleaders. Sometimes after practicing they'd put on their cheerleading uniforms—itchy wool sweaters worn by the girls who came before them—and cheer for the boys' basketball team.

Dance Hall Days

Friday nights were reserved for the weekly Police Association League dances held at Lewiston City Hall, where the police station was also housed at the time. They featured live bands—like the Royal Knights, who believably impersonated the Beatles—and drew up to two thousand fans weekly from the spring of 1964 to the end of November 1967.

Dorothy, her sister Peggy and their girlfriends would line up across from their dates, match up and stroll down the aisle between pairs. They'd shake their shoulders and wiggle their knees and sing along to the music. And if anybody gave one of her friends a hard time, Dorothy—tiny, but strong—would step in acting like she was six feet tall to protect them. Her posture and pointed words always prevented anything from getting physical, and they had fun. "If she liked you, you were golden. If not, not so good," shares Peggy, who admits her sister had a temper and could get feisty.

Beach Days

Teenagers in Sabattus hung out at sandy Long Beach on Sabattus Pond. At one and a half miles wide and three and a half miles long, the pond was so big people referred to it as a lake. On the beach was a building with a jukebox, pinball machines and wooden tables people would carve their initials in. The concession sold hamburgers, hotdogs, packaged ice creams, cotton candy and popcorn. There were changing stalls. Across the road was a small roller-skating rink. These days, the rink is closed, the beach stand gone and the pond so green with algae it's unthinkable for anyone to go swimming.

Terry Standley

Dorothy's first fervent crush was a charismatic blond-haired doe-eyed young seaman on the missile cruiser USS *William H. Standley*, which was being overhauled at the shipyard Bath Iron Works located in nearby Bath. She began dating Terry Standley (no relation to the ship's namesake Admiral William Harrison Standley) during her junior year, attending school and community dances together. At one point while the ship was inhabitable due to maintenance, he moved onto the Brunswick Naval Air Station base. Her family liked him. Several of her friends did too and also dated Brunswick sailors—the uniforms had an effect on them. During the one-week senior class trip to Washington, D.C., Philadelphia and New York City to see the monuments, Dorothy carried his photo in a card holder she placed on the nightstand by her bed in the hotel. She talked about him constantly. When the ship left Maine permanently, Dorothy was brokenhearted. Terry hitched up from Boston to see her a few times. Eventually, he went back home to Oregon.

Changing a Flat Tire

Out of all Dorothy's friends, she was the one who could be counted on to get them out of trouble. The time Sheila got a flat tire, there were five girls in the car and none of them could loosen the nuts on the rim. Dorothy took over and got it done. "We were on our way back from a dance hall," says Sue. "We were shocked to see her strength and relieved. It was in the middle of the night, and we were in the boonies."

BAD BOYS

Dorothy began spending time with Glenys, who was tougher and more jagged than her other friends in sixth grade. They would pass their days exploring in the woods, bicycling between their homes and swimming in a local pond on hot days.

Senior year with Glenys behind the wheel of her blue '62 Pontiac convertible, the two girls would drive to a supermarket parking lot in the neighboring town of Lisbon to hang out with mostly older boys who'd dropped out of school and were familiar to local law enforcement. These were the kind of guys Dorothy's other friends would avoid. They didn't just represent danger—they were in Lisbon, a town that shared an age-old rivalry with Sabattus. Only a decade earlier there had been street fights involving young people from each town.

During this time, Dorothy was lovesick over Terry, who'd be away for weeks with his ship out of port. Being a teenager, she wanted to have fun. She was also used to getting attention because she was beautiful and enjoyed the guys from Lisbon chasing her. And her other friends were busy—studying, working and taking care of their siblings.

One of the more rugged members of the Lisbon set, Gerald Arsenault was unremarkable save for his ability to make people feel uncomfortable. He was mean and dangerous and rarely sober, at least as a young man. Gerald was witnessed shooting a tree near where someone was standing. At an all-day parade in Lisbon Falls, he threw an exploding firework into a crowd of people. During both events, he was described as laughing hysterically.

According to sources, Gerald might also have been dealing drugs back then. He boasted freely of getting paid $1,500 (around $14,600 today) for making a "short walk one night and delivering a package."

Gerald was good buddies with Peter Milliken. In early 1967, Peter was seventeen going on twenty-one. He went from regularly attending church and Boy Scout troop meetings to a burgeoning delinquent with a growing rap sheet. He and Gerald drank a bit too much beer, drove a bit too fast and raised hell. There is a photo of them sporting plain T-shirts, holding cans of Budweiser and smiling, with cigarettes dangling from their mouths. The two men would remain friends for decades. Both would marry Dorothy.

Peter remembers meeting Dorothy for the first time. He was working on his brown-and-white '56 Buick four-door in the Tony Sunoco's parking lot in downtown Lisbon. Glenys was with Dorothy in the passenger seat. It was a sunny Sunday afternoon, and they wanted to know if Peter wanted to go for a ride with them. He did.

Looking back, Dorothy's senior year in high school was where her path began to divert from the one she'd been on toward something darker. It's as if she was running headlong into trouble, but what did she know about life and love? She was so young. Was this her cliff and she was jumping? Her life idling, her death a future headline. This was the late 1960s, and at that moment she had the last tiny taste of power she'd ever have.

THE WOMAN

In 1967, the summer after high school graduation, Sue and Dorothy shared a third-floor one-bedroom apartment walk-up on Bates Street in Lewiston. Terry had been hitchhiking up from whatever port he was in whenever he could but ultimately realized his attempts to keep the once so in love couple together were fruitless. He knew he'd eventually move back west and that Dorothy was not discouraging the Lisbon boys circling her.

The young women walked to work—Sue at the phone company and Dorothy at Kresge's department store—paid cheap rent and partied for three months.

"When she'd come to the apartment she'd have been drinking and walk in with a big rock," Sue says. "Every time. Wherever she went. I'd wake up in the morning and there'd be a big rock in the bed with sand on it. Dorothy lined them up—the rocks along the wall." Years later, when living with Peter, Dorothy would keep a bureau drawer full of rocks collected from everywhere she went.

"Because the town of Sabattus is so small and everybody knows everybody, when folks found out we had an apartment everybody went there," Sue shares. "People slept in bathtubs. It was fun." Except, that is, when Dorothy went out with her Lisbon friends—that was not Sue's kind of fun. They were too wild for her.

Dorothy and Sue would drink watered-down beers at local bars in Topsham and Brunswick. Their favorite place was the Heathwood, a large, smoky dance hall in Lisbon with live music. It was a hotspot in the 1970s, drawing in locals and sailors from the Brunswick Naval Air Station. Gerald and Peter also liked to drink there.

On July 5, 1967, Dorothy turned eighteen. That week, a little after midnight on Saturday, July 1, Gerald was driving alone in the lakeside town of Naples when he struck and killed a nineteen-year-old boy on the side of the road. He must have known he hit the teenager but continued down the road a few hundred yards to a camping area, where police found him. Gerald was booked at Cumberland County Jail in Portland on a charge of death caused by violation of law. He was released hours later on $1,500 bail. Within a week, he'd pleaded no contest—meaning he accepted conviction but did not admit guilt—to charges of reckless driving and leaving the scene of the accident. Ultimately, Gerald was fined $100 and received a six-month suspended reformatory sentence, and his license was suspended ten days.

Over the next year, he accumulated a list of violations ranging from littering on the highway to multiple charges of being intoxicated while operating a motor vehicle and possession of stolen property.

Meanwhile, on February 9, 1968, Dorothy fulfilled her dream of joining the military and enlisted in the Air Force. In high school, she wrote in her yearbook about her future plans

> to join the *WAVES* just to prove to people that the waves are a branch of the service that have something to be proud of and also [here college is crossed out] *to prove that they* [indecipherable word crossed out] *are not there for* [marriage is crossed out] *the sailors or officers to* [indecipherable word].

> *WAVES was an acronym for a branch of the U.S. Navy called Women Accepted for Volunteer Emergency Service that existed during World War II.

She spent about three months in basic training at Lackland Air Force Base located eleven miles west of San Antonio, Texas. According to Peggy, Dorothy hated Texas, telling her everything was brown, "even the toilet paper." When she returned to New England, she was stationed at Westover Air Base in Springfield, Massachusetts.

During this this time, she hitchhiked home and back to the base with her friend Sue Elbell. They'd get on the ramp, and Dorothy would stick out her thumb. She wasn't naïve but wouldn't think twice of taking a ride with anyone.

Marital Violence

There was no persuading Dorothy not to do something if she was determined, and she was fully committed to marrying Gerald Arsenault. When they got involved isn't clear, but on August 12, 1968, they eloped, becoming husband and wife.

Not long after they tied the knot, Dorothy became pregnant, her hitchhiking days behind her. Less than ten months after enlisting, on November 22, she was honorably discharged from Air Force. At the end of June 1969, Tonia was born. Dorothy doted on their daughter, but Tonia's birth did not improve Gerald or their relationship.

The marriage was predestined to be an unhappy one. Gerald was a flat-out drunk with a violent side. For him, maybe this was an attempt at a second chance at life. For her, family members think she wanted to redeem him. Friends can't make sense of it. Maybe, a few people said, it was because his badness appealed to her. Everyone pretty much concedes Dorothy liked a challenge and wasn't one to give up on someone. And everybody was concerned. Very concerned.

While the couple was living in an apartment up the hill from the Heathwood, an upstairs neighbor heard Dorothy calling for help. Responding, the neighbor found her alone, Gerald having made a fast retreat. Clumps of Dorothy's hair were on the kitchen floor. Tonia was in her crib in the bedroom.

Later, when living in a house on Main Street in Lisbon, Gerald broke windows while on a drunken rage while Tonia was in the room. It was the middle of winter.

A couple of Dorothy's friends recall her showing up to meet them sometime in 1970 covered in bruises. She didn't talk about it. Wouldn't complain. However, a few months later, she must have finally decided she'd had enough and left him. The divorce became official on June 15, 1971.

Around this time, Dorothy became a dental assistant for a family-owned practice based in Lewiston.

*Gerald died at the age of sixty-one in November 2008. The obituary read natural causes.

New Start

Meanwhile, Peter had married Glenys in June 1968, and they had two children before divorcing in July 1969.

Then one weekend in early 1971, Peter went out with Gerald and Dorothy to the Italian restaurant Graziano's Casa Mia. A local culinary institution in a rambling building, it was dark and decorated with boxing memorabilia. "Gerry was sitting there, and Dotty was sitting across from him and I was playing footsies with her," Peter shares. "Gerry says, 'I can see what you're doing.' And I said, 'I can't help it I still love Dotty.'" A few weeks later, Gerald and Dorothy filed for divorce and Peter and Dorothy got together.

If she was at all tentative about marrying Peter, there is no evidence. Photos from her June wedding day in 1973 show a glowing Dorothy huddled with her parents. She is wearing a feminine white ankle-length dress featuring puffy short sleeves paired with a wide-brimmed white sun hat with a long red ribbon.

Shortly after their marriage, they settled into their first home—an apartment on Shawmut Street in Lewiston. Peter, like Gerald, drank excessively. Her sisters and friends say Peter also cheated on Dorothy and that at least once she caught him in bed with another woman. Peter also ran with a tough crowd—guys who were known by the police. That group included his brother Dana, cousin Benny (would later fatally shoot his daughter's boyfriend), Randy Small (history of drunken driving in early 1970s), Lionel Lussier (would go on to receive multiple lengthy prison sentences) and Dorothy's ex and his longtime buddy Gerald.

On July 9, 1974, their blue-eyed dark-haired daughter Erica came into the world. And a little over two years later, on August 15, 1976, came Peter Arron Milliken, who became known as "little Pete." Both children were born at Central Maine General Hospital (now called Central Maine Medical Center) in Lewiston.

Peter was home for both births, but during the summers, he was making regular multiday trips for roofing and siding work to Presque Isle, a town several hours to the north. His older brother Dana had a home there, and during the 1970s he drove long haul all over the country. Occasionally, Peter says he would go on the road with Dana doing mechanical work on the truck. If it upset Dorothy that he was not home more she either didn't voice her concern to anyone or whoever she did confide in isn't telling.

*Little Pete died of natural causes at age thirty-eight on the morning of February 14, 2015, in Bangor, Maine.

Last Home

Six months before her death, Dorothy and Peter moved into her grandfather's old house on a narrow strand of rutted dirt road known as Pleasant Ridge Road. They didn't pay rent on the small home, but it lacked indoor plumbing and needed a lot of work to be livable. Peter rented a floor sander to repair the old pine floors, wallpapered and installed a heater, among other things. The front door opened into a low-ceilinged kitchen anchored by a wood stove. Under the room's one window was a pump sink and along one wall were built-in cabinets and open shelving made of a dark wood. Off that room was a living room, through which the two bedrooms were accessible. One for Peter and Dorothy—this is where little Pete slept—and one for Erica and Tonia. The murky rooms were lit by a few windows and lamps. An outhouse shed was accessible from the kitchen. The home was not an oppressive one, however, with a large yard for seven-year-old Tonia and two-year-old Erica to run around in.

It was uncommon for a house to not have plumbing at that time, even in a rural town. Though friends and neighbors wondered why Dorothy and Peter didn't live in a house closer to stores and amenities or at least one with indoor plumbing, they said nothing. Peggy says Dorothy didn't complain about living there and that she'd have preferred the peace of mind of not having rent to the conveniences.

Sleeping in the living room that fall was a nineteen-year-old by the name of Gail Ann Hinkley and her baby, Jeremy. Gail grew up on the Williams Road only about two hundred yards from the farm, and Dorothy had babysat her from time to time. Gail stood about 5'5" and had high cheekbones and a round face. She wore her brown, air-dried hair long. She'd been dating a guy she was crazy about, got pregnant and, when the father didn't want anything to do with the baby or her, needed a place to crash. Gail's childhood home was not an option—her mother had moved to Florida and she didn't get along with her father—so Dorothy offered her the sofa till she could get on her feet. They had an arrangement taking turns caring for each other's children.

THE NIGHT

Content warning: This section covers difficult topics, including violence and death.

T hat Friday, November 5, 1976, was going to be a busy one. Dorothy's maternity leave from the dentist's office was coming to an end, and the baby was scheduled for a minor surgery on Monday.

Just after daybreak, Dorothy went into the kitchen, pulled her yellow smiley face mug off the shelf and filled it with coffee. She then puttered around, getting Tonia's school lunch ready and clearing up. Peter was already up and out of the house. Most mornings he left for work by 7:00 a.m. and didn't return until 5:00 or 6:00 p.m.

Around 7:30 a.m., coffee in hand, Dorothy walked Tonia outside to meet the bus that would take her to Sabattus Elementary. She then went back inside, got dressed, drank the last bit of cold coffee, washed the mug, set it on the shelf, bundled up baby Pete and headed out the door, leaving Erica in Gail's care.

It was a bright day that was unseasonably warm with temperatures in the mid- to upper forties. A neighbor did yard work in a T-shirt. There were only a few houses scattered along the road, giving each a generous amount of space and privacy. After they'd moved into the area, Peter got to know the neighbors across the street and would advise them on mechanical stuff. Given how occupied Dorothy was with her children, housework and her job, it was harder for her to find time to do more than exchange pleasantries with them. That morning, she and the neighbor might have waved. He can't remember. It didn't seem important at the time.

Dorothy got in her 1968 white AMC Rambler American and drove to Mary Ellen's, where she dropped off Pete before heading to Lisbon or Lewiston to get her hair permed.

Midway through the school day, Dorothy picked Tonia up and took her to Mary Ellen's home in West Bowdoin. Tonia asked to stay over, and Dorothy agreed. The sisters took their coffees and sat down in the back doorway for a few minutes. This was the last time Mary Ellen would see her beloved sister.

Dorothy headed to Central Maine General Hospital with the baby for an appointment. She expected to meet Peter there, and when he didn't show, she was infuriated.

Temper Rising

Peter was making good money. He had a solid reputation as a hard worker who showed up on time, yet the family was still living pretty much hand to mouth. "Dotty would get so mad because it would be grocery money or whatever and his mother would come and say, 'I don't have no money,' and all she did with it was go out drinking." Peggy says. "He also spent a lot on alcohol and guns."

Late afternoon, Dorothy went to the farm to seek counsel from her parents. Peter, who had been drinking, showed up unannounced. His friend Randy Small had given him a ride, as Peter was without a car at the time. Their second car, a Chevrolet Vega, had broken down again or was repossessed depending on who you talk to. Dorothy and Peter argued for a bit, and while voices were raised, exactly what they were saying wasn't intelligible to the family. Eventually, Peter and Randy left to do some more drinking at the American Legion in Lisbon. While they were raising their beers, Dorothy took the baby home. She dressed herself in a white waist-length jacket, short-sleeve white shirt, jeans and her hallmark brown Dr. Scholl's sandals—and likely a chic belt that kind of hung down—as was her style.

Peter says he got home around 8:00 p.m., and Judy and Buggard Goddard, a couple of his friends, stopped by. Then after they left, he and Dorothy had dinner and he went to bed. He maintains he was unaware Dorothy left the house and had no idea she'd gone to the laundromat.

Dorothy's siblings have a different version of that evening. They say the Goddards stopped by briefly, and after they left, Dorothy and Peter had a vicious fight about his not having shown up for his son's doctor appointment and general lack of parental support. Mary Ellen says Gail Ann told her that the fight got physical, with Peter threatening to kill Dorothy and trying to rip little Pete out of her arms.

Mary Ellen also says Gail Ann told her that Peter was awake when Dorothy left the house.

The fight and possibly them making up delayed Dorothy's departure to the laundromat. Dorothy had been planning to go to the laundromat around 8:00 p.m., but it was closer to 10:30 p.m. when she loaded the bundles of laundry into her car. Before she left, she would have looked in on the children. Two-year-old Erica was on a cot in the bedroom and nearly three-month-old Pete in his crib in the adjacent room with his dad. Dorothy then closed the door of the house behind her for the final time. She backed down the driveway, the tires of her car making a crunching sound as she turned onto the road.

A Familiar Sight

At her childhood home, she went through the door into the kitchen. Dorothy had gone to the farm to see if her mother, who usually accompanied her to the laundromat in the evening, would go with her, but she was not feeling well.

She sat with her father on a sofa drinking coffee and talking with him for a while. Dorothy was so tired and sad. Ronaldo watched his worried daughter. He hated to see her this way. She told him how the hospital was pressing her to pay her bills for an accident Erica had that May when she broke her arm and for baby Pete's delivery, how she had no support from Peter and felt like she was taking the whole brunt of it all. He might have patted her head and reassured her in his soft voice, looked her straight in the eye and advised her. Inside he was raging.

As they were talking, Dorothy realized how late it had gotten and asked her father if he could go with her to the laundromat. He said no, a response that would weigh on him for the rest of his life. After a few more minutes, she said her goodbyes and got into her car. It was probably around 11:30 p.m. when she departed, possibly later.

The haze of yellow light shone through from the windows and the sky was full of stars as she walked the brief well-worn path from the house to her car. She turned the key in the ignition, put pressure on the gas and drove down lightless rural roads, eventually turning onto the two-lane blacktop road Lisbon Street (Maine State Route 196) in Lewiston.

Sometime presumably before midnight, Dorothy pulled up to the corner of Dumont Avenue where the Beal's Laundromat was located. The glare of her car lights reflected on the glass front of the laundromat as she pulled into the parking lot. After she turned off the car's ignition, she might have sat for a few minutes and looked around before sliding out of the driver's seat.

When Dorothy went inside, she wouldn't have been surprised that no one was there. She emptied her box of detergent in the washers and loaded them with quarters. At some point, unless she brought it from home, she might have walked across the street to Healy's Garage to get a can of Pepsi from the soda vending machine.

As she sucked on her Virginia Slims cigarette and sipped her Pepsi, she'd have used the quiet to think about choices she had to make, things that needed doing. After a couple of hours, she lifted her clothes out of the dryer and began folding them on one of the tables in the middle of the room. Then she was interrupted. Did she look out into the parking lot and see a friendly face, or was there a tap, tap, tap on the glass front door by a stranger? Or perhaps did a person she'd seen around town, but didn't know—at least by name—come in the side door to use the only (public) bathroom around after a night of drinking?

The End and the Beginning

Whatever the reason, at some point, Dorothy left the building and went into the chilled air of the parking lot, leaving her jacket behind on the counter. She'd have been shivering in her flimsy top. Seconds or minutes later, a hand abruptly reached out, grabbing her by the arm, and suddenly the man's fists began raining down on her face. Then he pulled a large metal object out from somewhere. He swung, and she fought against him, surely her muscles burning the adrenaline coursing through her veins, the need to survive for her children. She raised her hands in a futile effort to protect her face. He swung again, breaking every bone in one of her perfectly manicured hands. She'd have staggered backward confused, panic rising, her bloodcurdling screams ignored. Her voice echoing into the otherwise still night.

She tried to get away, one of her wood sandals clunking on the ground. There was no escaping. He was too strong, too determined. Her knees buckled, unable to recover her balance. Another swing—this one to the right side of her forehead—and she slumped down on the ground. The whole attack might have taken one or two long minutes. Brief, excessive and lethal.

The killer dragged her to the side of the building and propped her up. He then either went inside to the little back corner bathroom and wiped the blood off his hands or fled to a waiting car thinking about where to dispose of the bloody tool.

One might recall the infamous story from 1964 of Kitty Genovese, the young woman stabbed to death in front of her apartment building in Queens, New York, as dozens of neighbors did nothing. Their bedroom lights turned on, actually interrupting the perpetrator between multiple attacks. When woken from sleep, did they understand what they were hearing? Were her desperate cries for help confused for a lover's quarrel? Did history repeat itself in Lewiston in 1976? Was this yet another example of witness apathy, when indifferent neighbors in apartment buildings sandwiching the laundromat listened—maybe even watched—and did nothing? Did anyone call the Lewiston police? Did the dispatch officer at police headquarters at 27 Pine Street pick up?

Regardless, the results were that the end of a long night saw the lifeless body of a mother with extraordinary grieving yet to come. The laundromat was empty. The night silent.

Decades later, a woman stopped by the business housed where the laundromat used to be and proudly shared that from her window, she had seen the dead body of Dorothy Milliken lying there. She was there to gossip, to claim her spot in the executioner's balcony.

CHRONOLOGY OF DOROTHY'S LAST MOVEMENTS

Friday, November 5

6:30 a.m.	Dorothy is up and prepping for the day
7:00 a.m.	By this time, Peter has left the house for work.
7:30 a.m.	Around this time, Dorothy walks Tonia outside to meet the bus that would take her to Sabattus Elementary. School begins at 8:15 a.m.
8:30 a.m.–9:30 a.m.	Dorothy takes the baby—little Pete—to her sister Mary Ellen's in West Bowdoin. Gail stays home with her son and Erica.
9:00 a.m.–11:00 a.m.	Dorothy gets her hair permed in Lisbon or Lewiston.
12:30 p.m.–1:30 p.m.	Dorothy picks Tonia up at school and takes her to Mary Ellen's. The sisters have coffee, and Dorothy agrees to let Tonia stay over there.

At some point after seeing Mary Ellen, before heading to the hospital, it's possible Dorothy met up with a friend in Lisbon or Lewiston.

THE MURDER

of

DOROTHY MILLIKEN

Cold Case in Maine

Sharon Kitchens

THE History PRESS

THE MURDER OF DOROTHY MILLIKEN
Cold Case in Maine
BY SHARON KITCHENS

9781467159449 {$24.99}

On November 5, 1976, twenty-seven-year-old Dorothy Milliken left her rural home in Sabattus, Maine, to go to an all-night laundromat. The following morning, her body was found slumped against the outside wall. Despite various leads, there were no arrests for her murder. Dorothy Milliken became a name typed on an index card filed at state police headquarters, her crime scene displayed in grainy black-and-white photos in the evening newspapers. Nearly five decades later, author Sharon Kitchens examines the cold case, interviewing more than forty people, including Dorothy's family, friends, former neighbors, law enforcement and forensic specialists. Who was Dorothy? Why has her killer never been found? Did she know her murderer, or was her death due to a random, frenzied attack?

A portion of the profits from the sale of the book are being donated to the Forensic Anthropology Identification and Recovery (FAIR) Lab at the University of New Hampshire. The FAIR Lab trains students to excavate, recover and identify human remains.

Hi Cindy —

Thanks for reading Dorothy's story.

Take care, Sharon X

happy for you!!!

p.s. Soooooo

1:30 p.m.–3:30 p.m.	Dorothy heads to Central Maine General Hospital in Lewiston for little Pete's appointment. The baby has his appointment. Peter is a no-show.
3:30 p.m.–5:30 p.m.	Dorothy goes to the farm in Sabattus to talk to her parents. Peter and his buddy Randy Small, both of whom have been drinking, show up unannounced. Dorothy and Peter are seen arguing.
5:30 p.m.–7:30 p.m.	Peter and Randy go to the American Legion Hall in Lisbon. Dorothy heads home with the baby. She changes her clothes and takes care of the kids. Gail is home.
7:30 p.m.–8:30 p.m.	Randy drops Peter off at his home around this time. Peter's friends Judy and Buggard Goddard stop by. They visit for around thirty minutes.
8:30 p.m.–10:30 p.m.	Dorothy and Peter renew their fight from earlier in the day. According to Gail Ann, the fight got physical with Peter threatening to kill Dorothy.
10:30 p.m.–10:45 p.m.	Dorothy puts several bundles of laundry in the car and heads to the farm. Peter says he is asleep and doesn't know Dorothy left the house or where she went.
11:00 p.m.	Dorothy arrives at the farm and has a cup of coffee with her dad. She asks both parents if either can accompany her to the laundromat. Neither is able to.
11:45 p.m.–midnight	Dorothy pulls up to Beal's Laundromat at 969 Lisbon Street. It's possible she stopped to get gas and a Pepsi at Healy's Garage diagonally across the street.

Saturday, November 6

After 2:30 a.m.

Investigators initially estimate Dorothy's time of death as sometime after 2:30 a.m. The medical examiner stated she was killed in the early morning hours.

4:45 a.m.

A young man dropping off papers on the sidewalk in front of the laundromat finds Dorothy's body by the side door on Dumont Avenue.

Teenage Dorothy Milliken (1966) and her grandmother Dorothy (St. Onge) Rancourt, who she was named after, in her early twenties, circa 1915. *Courtesy of the Rancourt family.*

George "Ronaldo" Rancourt in his late twenties (*right*). *Courtesy of the Rancourt family.*

Top: Dorothy's childhood home in Sabattus. *Courtesy of the Rancourt family*.

Bottom: Ronaldo with daughters Dorothy and Mary Ellen, early 1950s. *Courtesy of the Rancourt family*.

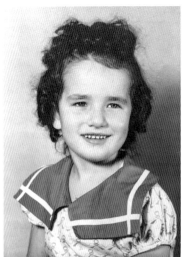

Above: Dorothy age seventeen. *Courtesy of the Rancourt family.*

Left: Dorothy at age two. *Courtesy of the Rancourt family.*

Below: Sabattus High School, where Dorothy graduated from in 1967. *Source unknown, Sabattus Historical Society.*

Above: The Sabattus High Squaws, the girls' basketball team. Dorothy and some of her close friends played two or more years. *From the 1966 edition of the Sabattus High School yearbook.*

Right: Dorothy "Dotty" and friends their senior year of high school. *Courtesy of the Rancourt family.*

JACKIE CEO. MAY · 67 DOTTIE SHELIA

LEO DIANA GLENDA DANNY

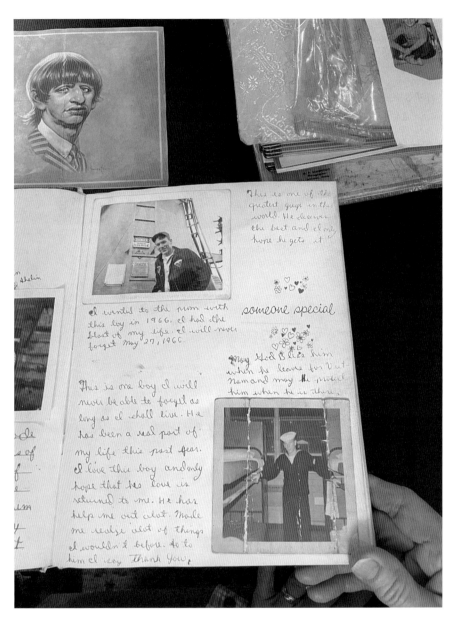

Images of young sailor Terry Standley, then Dorothy's boyfriend, along with her handwriting in her high school senior year memory book. It's possible Dorothy took at least one of these photos. *Courtesy of the Rancourt family.*

dates to remember

This is one night that I shall never forget for the rest of my life. It was my first date with Terry and it was truly the most fun I had ever had. This night brought my real first love in my life.

I do love him

Terrance Glen Standley

Remember the day you got your first car, first formal gown? Remember the date you were accepted by the college of your choice or for your first full-time job? You won't remember if you don't jot them down on these pages . . . and use a photograph or other memento to help you recall. This is the time of life when many momentous things will be happening to you: don't let them slip by unrecorded.

Images of young sailor Terry Standley, then Dorothy's boyfriend, in her high school senior year memory book. Photographer unknown. *Courtesy of the Rancourt family.*

Above: Dorothy and Peter's wedding day. Peter's sister is helping Dorothy get ready. *Courtesy of the Rancourt family*.

Opposite, top: Dorothy's future husbands Peter Milliken (in the white T-shirt) and Gerald Arsenault (in the black T-shirt). Photographer unknown. *Courtesy of the Rancourt family*.

Opposite, bottom: Dorothy and her parents on her wedding day in June 1973. *Courtesy of the Rancourt family*.

Top: Dorothy and Peter Milliken, June 1973. *Courtesy of the Rancourt family*.

Bottom: A birthday card from Dorothy to Tonia in June 1971 on her second birthday. Dorothy was visiting Peter in Aroostook County, where he was working with his brother. *Courtesy of the Rancourt family*.

Early morning photo of Dorothy's car parked in front of the Beal's Laundromat. *Courtesy of the Sun Journal.*

Lewiston police readying Dorothy's car to be towed to the impound lot. *Courtesy of the Sun Journal; photo by Simokaitis.*

Scene of the crime at Beal's Laundromat in Lewiston on November 6, 1976. *Courtesy of the Sun Journal; photo by Simokaitis.*

Dorothy's route
From the FARM to
BEAL'S LAUNDROMAT

11/5/76

Williams Road
↓
Bowdoinham Road
↓
Crowley Road
↓
South Lisbon Road
↓
Lisbon Street /196

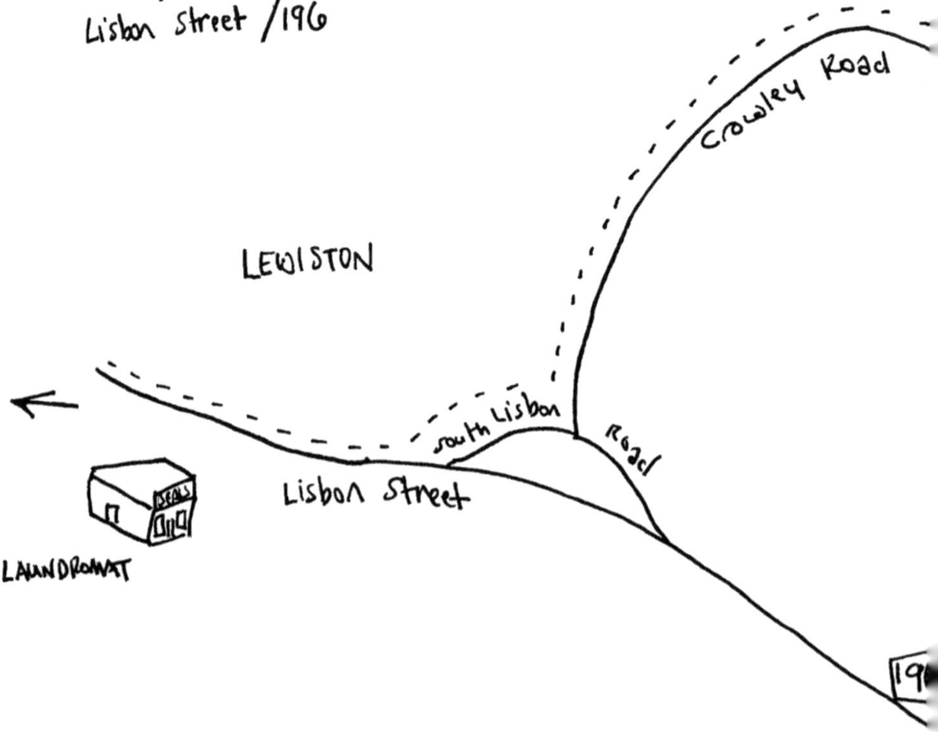

Crowley Road

LEWISTON

South Lisbon
Road

Lisbon Street

LAUNDROMAT

BEALS

196

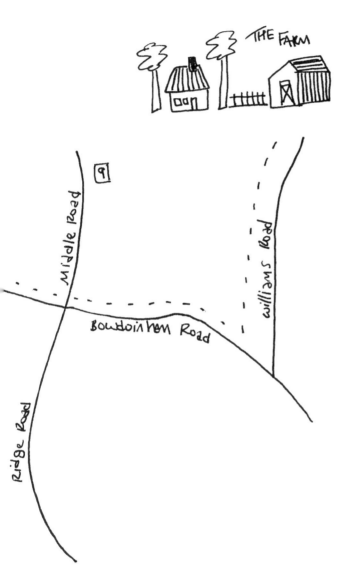

Hand-drawn map of the route Dorothy would have taken from the farm (where her parents lived) in Sabattus) to Beal's Laundromat in Lewiston. *Map by author.*

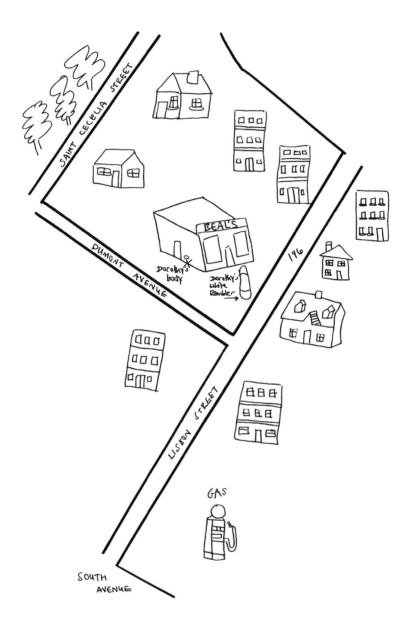

Hand-drawn map of Dorothy's crime scene. *Map by author.*

2

A MURDER INVESTIGATION

MORNING WATCH

It was around 4:45 a.m. on Saturday, November 6, when a young man dropping off papers on the sidewalk in front of 969 Lisbon Street noticed something by the side door on Dumont Avenue. At first, he might have thought it was a sleeping bag, even though it would have been rare to find a destitute person in that area at that time. As he stepped closer and stared down, he would have realized it was the body of a petite woman crumpled on the ground, one sandal lying beside her. Her blood in the glow of the moonlight might have looked like oil. What he saw affected him deeply for a long while after.

It took him about ten minutes in the bitter cold to flag down a Lewiston police officer in a car. A man walking his dog passed by around this time. The police dispatcher on duty noted the call for assistance came in at 4:57 a.m.

Walkie-talkies were a precious commodity and prioritized for men walking the beat. Car men had radios attached to their cars. If a car man had to get out at a scene, he could switch the radio in the cruiser to PA Mode to hear what was going on but while separated from his car could not communicate.

When the first patrol officer pulled up to Dorothy's crime scene, protocol would have dictated that even if he had to drive a few blocks, he was supposed to find a beat man before getting out of the car to view her body. Then they'd both get out so they were always in contact with the station. A former Lewiston officer explaining this says it seems kind of strange, but that's how it worked.

First on the Scene

The first uniformed officers on the scene must have been shaken. You just didn't see brutalized dead women like this in Lewiston. When Sergeant Roger Bisson arrived shortly after they did, he'd have visually checked on Dorothy and presumably made a sweep of the laundromat to ensure the killer wasn't still inside. In his fourteen years on the force, Bisson had seen dead bodies but almost assuredly nothing compared to what he saw that morning. As a member of Lewiston's six-member detective team, he was used to investigating robberies, drug deals, sexual assaults and cases of domestic violence. This was out of his purview.

Bisson had an uneasy feeling about that scene. Originally, he thought that her throat had been slashed and the body mutilated. Dorothy's white shirt would likely have been covered in blood from wounds.

The police radio crackled. Local detectives were called out of bed. Soon patrol cars with their blue lights flashing headed to the address, where a crime scene awaited. The sky was still dark outside.

Boys in Blue

The Lewiston cops who arrived to secure the scene wore dark blue pants and light blue shirts with dark blue trim underneath lightly insulated cruiser jackets. Their wool caps with shearling-lined earflaps were much appreciated in the biting cold. They placed folding barricades along Lisbon Street and awaited their orders. In the meantime, an ambulance with first-aid responders would have shown up.

At the time, a routine week in Lewiston for the local cops consisted of petty theft, citations for drunk driving and speeding, public intoxication, domestic disturbances, bar fights and burglaries. A murder—especially one as violent and public as Dorothy's—would have drawn a crowd of law enforcement officers, not all directly involved with the investigation. Higher-ups, Police Chief Lucien Longtin and District Attorney Thomas Delahanty II among them, made the short drive up Lisbon Street from city hall downtown to the laundromat.

Word of the murder would have traveled quickly around Lewiston and Auburn, located just across the Androscoggin River. If you'd driven by the laundromat that morning, you'd have seen every press outlet from as far as Portland and Bangor jostling to get a photograph, get information. A block up at Bonneau's Supermarket, you might have overheard shocked, curious customers and checkout staff trying to process what had happened.

The cluster of boys in blue on Morning Watch had their work cut out for them. They'd been on duty since 12:30 a.m. and almost certainly would be working well past the scheduled end of their day at 8:30 a.m.

On Duty

The following Lewiston police were assigned the midnight to 8:00 a.m. shift known as "Morning Watch" between September and November 1976:

Captain Gerard Laroche, Lieutenant Roy Perham and Sergeant Thomas Carey

Richard Nicolazzo, Richard Grondin, Ernest Carrier and James Roberge were assigned to the Main and Lisbon Street beats. It's possible they were called off these to assist.

Cars were manned by Jonathan Pyska*, Gerald Patterson, Richard Roberts, Kenneth Gilman*, Matthew Grenham, Richard Cloutier and Edgar Lizotte.

Gerard Baril was the dispatcher.

Swing beat men were Ronald LaFlamme, Max Ashburn, Dennis Paquin and Donald Mondor.

*Jonathan Pyska had been with the force a year or two at that time. Years later, he would tell Dorothy's daughter Tonia, "Blue protects blue." A former colleague says he used to talk about Dorothy's murder all the time. It's unconfirmed whether he was on duty that morning.

*Kenneth Gilman was not on duty that morning.

Increase in Violent Crime

About one hour after the local authorities were on the scene, the state police began arriving. Since 1968, they've had primary jurisdiction over homicide cases with the exceptions of those occurring in the Portland and Bangor areas.

In the 1970s, the Maine State Police Criminal Division's Bureau of Criminal Investigation (BCI) ran all of the state-designated homicide investigations. At that time, the BCI was composed of three divisions of seven to eight investigators each. The Northern Division was based in Orono and responsible for Hancock, Washington, Aroostook, Piscataquis and Penobscot (where Bangor is) Counties. The Central Division was in charge of Kennebec, Waldo, Somerset, Knox, Lincoln and Sagadahoc Counties. The Southern Division was based in Scarborough and in charge of York, Cumberland (where Portland is), Androscoggin (where Lewiston is), Oxford and Franklin Counties. *Today the state's criminal investigation division is known as the Major Crime Unit. The geographic distribution is roughly the same.

ACCORDING TO THE FEDERAL Bureau of Investigation in 1971, there were twenty homicides in Maine. The most ever was fifty-five in 1972. In 1973, there were twenty-two, in 1974 and 1975 each there were thirty. There were twenty-nine murders in Maine in 1976. During the first part of 1976, the state had one of the lowest periods of homicides in five years. Then in October, the state police investigated fifteen homicides, the most concentrated in Maine's history.

Prior to the mid-1970s, three-quarters of Maine homicides were domestic disputes between two people who knew each other. Authorities did not know what was causing the "surge" in what they referred to as unprovoked stranger killings.

The country as a whole was experiencing economic challenges, widespread drug use, urban development—in Lewiston this looked more like restructuring—and changing social dynamics. Societal attitudes toward violence were showcased with the popularity of films like John Carpenter's *Assault on Precinct 13* and Clint Eastwood's *Dirty Harry* series. News programs and newspapers emphasized the most dramatic effects of violent crimes. Serial killers like Edmund Kemper, the "Co-Ed Killer," and John Wayne Gacy, the "Killer Clown" were semiregular front-page news.

But public perception in Maine was that those events were far away in big cities. This was Maine, a rural state made up of classic small towns with family businesses where neighbors know neighbors and charming lakeside communities with mountain trails leading out of people's backyards. It was not supposed to be the kind of place where young women go out to buy cough syrup and never come home or take a shortcut they've taken a thousand times before and end up taking their last breath, or where you're interrupted folding your newborn's cloth diapers in a laundromat and beaten to death in the parking lot.

On April 4, seven months before Dorothy was murdered, a partially clad twenty-seven-year-old woman from neighboring Lisbon Falls was found beaten to death in her ground-floor apartment kitchen by her four-year-old son. The autopsy results revealed she had died of head injuries. Burglary was not considered a motive, as nothing was reported missing.

In Maine, people might have bought guns or dogs and there was an edge not present before, but they largely still left their doors unlocked.

Law and Order

Detective Willard Parker of the state police headed the investigation the first week. By 1976, he'd been on the job around nineteen years and knew the Lewiston area well. Former colleague Lyndon Abbott, who was good friends with Parker, says he was an exceptional interviewer, but because he served as a security officer for the governor, he had not seen a lot of homicide scenes. According to Abbott, James Pinette, who was on the scene in a supportive capacity, also lacked crime scene management training.

Parker was still a trooper when he completed a two-week Criminal Investigative Course at the Maine Criminal Justice Academy eight months earlier. The curriculum included rules of evidence, polygraph procedures, state police laboratory services, interviewing and interrogation, forensic medicine, homicide investigation, planning major arrests and arson investigation. Sometime between early February and early November 1976, he achieved the rank of detective. Bruce Rafnell, who would take Dorothy's case over in mid-November 1976, was enrolled in the course with Parker and also became a detective in the months leading up to Dorothy's murder.

It's possible Parker and Pinette were the only officers available that day in that area and that's why they were temporarily assigned to it. Normally, detectives initially assigned to a case see it through. It's unknown if Rafnell was on the scene that day. He was still working the unsolved Lisbon Falls homicide from April and would receive another local short-term assignment later that day.

Evidence Collection

Due to inexperience and intimidation, Lewiston police allowed a number of higher-ups and possibly even members of the press to traipse onto the scene, thus contaminating it.

It was the job of Peter McCarthy, with the state's crime lab, to photograph, gather and log evidence that day. If he didn't do the job correctly, evidence might not be admissible in court. In the 1970s, police protocol didn't dictate that they wear protective clothing or footwear. However, he would have been wearing gloves.

Scene-of-crime kit in hand, he made his way to Dorothy's body. He'd have examined her visually, as only the state's medical examiner was supposed to touch her. At some point, her hands were placed in plastic bags.

His assumption was this was a personal crime, a hunch McCarthy felt confirmed once he surveyed the interior of the laundromat and found no signs of a struggle. Dorothy's neatly folded laundry sat on the table; nothing was knocked over. There were no scuff marks. Her wallet containing $200 was inside the pocketbook on the counter. Considering this, robbery was dismissed as the motive. A theory began forming in his mind that this was a lover's quarrel, maybe an enraged husband. He reasoned, why else would she have walked outside into the darkness?

The Cash

There is a question regarding where the cash came from. Though it was not stolen when Dorothy was killed, the police asked about it in at least two interviews. In 1976, $200 has a purchasing power of about $1,106 in 2024. That's obviously a lot of money to be carrying around, especially if you're married to someone you already feel you have to hide money from—which Dorothy did. Mary Ellen says Peter found her stash of cash at least once—money Dorothy intended for groceries and household bills—and took it.

Peggy believes the cash was a result of a Beeline Fashions home show Mary Ellen had hosted at the end of October. Beeline was a popular company that made trendy ready-to-wear clothes and recruited housewives who'd invite friends and neighbors over to check out the latest styles and place orders from books with the designs and swatches of fabric. In exchange for their efforts, the hostesses received a commission or company credit for clothes. According to Beeline company policy, Mary Ellen was supposed to collect and send in the money for orders within two to three weeks of the party.

Peggy thinks the reason Dorothy had that much cash on her is because she'd invited friends from Lisbon to the party and was in the process of collecting their money for orders when she was killed. That maybe she'd met up with someone earlier that day after seeing Mary Ellen and still had other friends to collect from.

Ignored Crime Scenes

Because of the state of the interior, only the parking lot was treated as a scene and processed thoroughly. Dorothy's car was towed to the impound lot. It would be released to Peter Milliken a week later. When he picked it up, he did not notice any black fingerprint powder, meaning it also was not processed as a crime scene. No one may ever know how much potential evidence was missed because the inside of the laundromat and Dorothy's car were ignored at a forensic level.

Abbott, at one time one of the state's leading homicide men, describes McCarthy as meticulous and capable of tremendous results with toolmark examinations. He says McCarthy was not an expert with bloodwork and fingerprinting. Abbott explains that if it was a real whodunit scene like Dorothy's was shaping up to be that day, he'd have had all four guys from the lab or at least two on the scene. Sometimes it would happen due to availability, that only one lab man would be available, as was the case that day.

Abbott says—clarifying this didn't necessarily apply to McCarthy that day—that if you're an expert at something you want to be called into a case requiring your expertise, that you might not be too happy to do everything. Especially if you're the head of the group.

"Let's Not Confuse That with the Facts"

Dale Ames, a state police legend, frequently partnered with Abbott on investigations. He was known as a tremendous scene man, digging deeper and going wider than anyone else. His catchphrase was "Let's not confuse that with the facts," meaning don't make assumptions, follow what the evidence says and document it as such.

He once helped solve a homicide with candle wax. In December 1973, Jack and Florence Bettencourt, the owners of a secondhand store, were shot in their home in Liberty, Maine. When the car of one of the suspects was located, Ames worked on it for three days. He found traces of candle wax under an armrest. It turns out there'd been a thunderstorm that night and the power went out. The killers took candles from the house for light to find their way. Authorities were able to prove the wax in the car came from the candles in the house.

Sometimes Ames would go with Pete McCarthy to a scene, Ames as the detective, McCarthy as the lab tech. In that environment, Abbott describes McCarthy as being very successful.

Your Best Witness

Homicide detectives say every crime scene investigation should start with the body—it's your best witness.

While McCarthy and other investigators worked the scene, the chief medical examiner for the state, Dr. Henry Ryan arrived in his trademark khakis and rumpled blue suit coat under a gray trench coat with a clipboard under one arm and a pipe likely in hand. He was fresh on the job but already respected—a respect that would only grow during his twenty-two-year tenure. It was his job to coax whatever clues remained from Dorothy's body.

Dr. Ryan's presence reassured many in law enforcement. He was serious, empathetic and smart as heck but also jovial. And he had a reputation for being very thorough.

On entering the scene, he would have spoken with Detective Willard before looking at Dorothy's body. Then he would have walked around her body before going in for a closer look—studying her exposed skin for discoloration, looking at her wounds and moving her fingers and maybe one of her legs, to check for stiffness that would indicate the onset of rigor mortis and help him determine possible time of death. He also likely took his own photos as he sometimes did at scenes. Depending on how experienced the detectives were with crime scene investigation, he might have looked around further.

MAKING NOTIFICATIONS

Just after sunrise, a deputy from the Androscoggin County Sheriff's Office pulled up to the farmhouse facing the Millikens' on Pleasant Ridge Road, mistakenly thinking that was where he'd find Peter. Correctly interpreting the inhabitants of the house were still asleep, he tapped the siren to wake them up. He then got out of the car and knocked on the door. The surprised neighbors opened the door to a man in a brown uniform inquiring if this was the Milliken household. "No, it's across the street," the neighbors told him. When it was clear something had happened to Dorothy, they asked if there'd been a car accident. The sheriff's deputy made it clear there had not been. It was something far more nefarious than that, he assured them. Dorothy had been killed. And with that, he walked back to his car, got in and moved it across the street.

Meanwhile, Lionel Cote, who had known Peter for a number of years—having arrested him on more than one occasion for traffic violations and possession of alcohol when he was a wayward youth—knocked on the correct door. In 1976, Cote was wearing both the Androscoggin County sheriff's hat and that of the chief of Sabattus police. Cote likely knew Dorothy, at least by sight—so would some of the Lewiston officers on the scene. For a short while in her early twenties, she had waitressed for a popular Italian sandwich and pizza place called Mario's that was owned by two Lewiston officers.

"He told me something had happened to my wife and then they asked me to come with them," Peter recalls. "There was a girl staying with us at the time so I said, 'Ok you watch the kids while I go to Lewiston.' They wouldn't even tell me anything until we got up to where the scene was."

After Peter was notified, the sheriff or one of his deputies went back across the street to the neighbors and asked someone to go over to the house. It's unclear if this request came from Cote or was prompted by Peter. The wife crossed the street and entered into something she likens to a scene from a horror movie. Peter was in the corner of the kitchen on the floor sobbing with Erica on his lap rocking back and forth. Gail (whom Peter refers to as "the girl") was there, as were police officers (she's not sure if they were from the sheriff's office or Sabattus police). She had no idea why someone wanted her there, and all she wanted to do was get away.

Peter was driven (he doesn't remember by whom—if it was the Lewiston or Sabattus police or sheriff's deputies) to Lewiston to identify the body. Rather than bring him on the scene, they took him to the gas station located across the street and down part of a block. He could see her body covered up and her car at the laundromat. The police told him Dorothy had been beaten to death.

"I couldn't go over there," he says. "They asked me if I wanted to identify her." He refused to do the identification and asked them to contact his brother-in-law Moe, who was living in Lewiston. He also told the authorities he had no idea Dorothy had left the house to go to laundry. The fact that he refused to identify the body personally raised a flag for at least Peter McCarthy, who remains confident there is no way Peter didn't know his wife had left the house or know where she'd gone.

As Peter was being taken home, Dorothy's body was zipped into a body bag and placed in an ambulance.

Body Identification

Dorothy's sister Peggy was home alone when she says two Lewiston police officers knocked on her door asking to speak to her husband, Moe. Although it was early on a Saturday morning, Moe wasn't home, and this being before the age of cellphones, she couldn't just call him. His father owned an excavation, paving and plowing business down the road. Peggy told the officers the last she knew he was there. They left, and she waited for what she says felt like an eternity.

Moe, meanwhile, was driving a bulldozer down the side of the road. "I start backing up and I hear the blues," he recalls. "I thought they're going to nail me for going up the side of the road with the bulldozer. They come out of the car and say, 'Do you know Dorothy Milliken?' and I said, 'Yes,' and they said well you've been picked to identify her on the scene. I said, 'What'd she do get in a car accident?' They said, 'We can't tell you anything,' so I got in the back seat and they drove me to Beal's Laundromat."

During the several minutes it took to get to the scene, Moe asked the officers why the husband didn't do the identification and why he was picked. He says they didn't talk to him at all.

At the scene, the uniformed officers walked him up to the ambulance parked in front of the laundromat. Someone (he cannot recall who) pulled back the white blanket covering her. They asked him if that was Dorothy Milliken. He said, "Yes." They said, "Alright that's it." He remembers seeing that she had blood around her head and imprints on her arm from the tool used to beat her. "She wasn't cleaned up," he shares. "Put it that way."

After the identification, the police gave Moe a ride home, where he notified Peggy.

Informing the Parents

While Moe was doing the identification, Cote went to tell Dorothy's parents. Dorothy's younger brother, George, recalls his father sitting in the wooden rocking chair in the kitchen. His mother was across the room. George says initially his mother thought Dorothy had had a breakdown because she had been so stressed about the baby being sick, bills and Peter being "the way he was." She also knew Dorothy had been staying home a lot and keeping to herself. One state investigator wondered if Dorothy had postpartum depression. If she was dealing with depression and/or anxiety, there is no clinical proof the family is aware of.

Pépère was asleep in his bedroom during the notification. The family says when he found out, he was distraught.

Ronaldo went to Mary Ellen's. She can remember her husband coming through the bedroom door. "I woke right up," she says. "He said something about my dad wanting to talk to me, and I can remember jumping out of the bed and putting pants on and my dad coming in and he said, 'I have some bad news.' Something about somebody's death. And the first thing that came to my mind was my grandfather Pépère. He said no, and then when he said my sister, I just lost it."

Tonia remembers waking up at 2:30 maybe 3:00 a.m. and telling her cousin Julie that an angel had just come to her and that something was wrong and she didn't know what. "Then I remember sitting downstairs at my aunt Mary's house and my grandfather walking through the door and him coming to me," she recalls. "He said your mother or I can't remember exactly what he said something happened to your mom and I said, 'It's OK, Grandpa I already know,' and then I remember him going into my aunt Mary's room and telling her and I remember my aunt Mary losing her shit. I don't think I ever heard anybody scream as loud as she did and I think she knocked her bureau over. And that's when I think I shut down because of her reaction. That moment that trauma killed everything else."

Tonia has tried her hardest to remember details about her mother, but after that morning, she can recall only bits and pieces. Decades on, it's hard at times for her to decipher between what is a real memory and something someone told her.

After Ronaldo left Mary Ellen's, he disappeared for a few hours. George thinks he went looking for Gerald Arsenault, because his father knew he had threatened Dorothy when they were married. "He had supposedly bought silver bullets for him, Pete and her," George says. "But they checked him out, and he had an absolute alibi." The siblings have never really suspected Gerald because he and Dorothy had been divorced for a few years and because Dorothy was beaten not shot.

When he returned home, Peggy says the twinkle went out of her father's eyes. "The thing he'd been most afraid of was one of his children getting hurt," she shares.

THE DAY SHIFT

Shortly before 9:00 a.m., Dorothy's body arrived at Augusta General Hospital thirty miles to the north, where Dr. Ryan had his office.

Around this time, the small, gray-haired body of sixty-nine-year-old Robert "Shorty" McBride of Sanford, Maine, was found on a cot in his small room on the second floor of the green-trimmed yellow horse barn at the Lewiston Fairgrounds. He had likely been passed out lying face down when beaten to death with a wooden two-by-four sometime in the early morning hours.

The combined cases were sure to get local and state coverage. When word got out, this would have long-lasting ripple effects on the community—the second brutal murder in a twenty-four-hour span.

Many, including uniformed and city detectives, Chief Longtin, DA Delahanty II, sheriff's deputies and the state police investigators, left Dorothy's crime scene to examine McBride's.

Pressure

A basic rule to a murder investigation is that after the first twenty-four to forty-eight hours, the chances of solving a case begin to grow slimmer. More than just the need to move quickly associated with securing and processing a homicide crime scene, local and state law enforcement would have felt a real sense of urgency. It was unprecedented to have two murders in a twenty-four-hour period in a town where it was common to leave one's keys in their unlocked car.

It was all-hands-on-deck for the six members of Lewiston Police Department's detective bureau, who would be asked by the state homicide guys to check on specific things. Their community knowledge and informants could be invaluable at unburying secrets. How much they actually helped, however, is debatable.

A Different Truth

Two days into the investigation, DA Delahanty II praised the Lewiston police for being "extremely cooperative" with the state police on recent investigations. "One of the most important facets of an investigation like this is the initial protection of the scene," the DA shared. "And this was done in a most efficient manner."

Interviews with former members of the Lewiston police and state police convey a different truth. In reality, the former eyed the latter as interlopers, and local officers were none too eager to go out of their way to assist on a homicide investigation. They would've seen the state police as bigfooting a case where they felt they had jurisdiction. That resentfulness could lead to information being held back. Chief Longtin was especially known for being uncooperative when it came to having the state police in his backyard. He liked to do things his way.

Did You See or Hear Anything?

A primary tool available to law enforcement in 1976 was shoe leather and getting off one's ass and knocking on doors of people who lived in the immediate vicinity of the laundromat. Lewiston police fanned out, asking residents their full name, whether they were home Friday night, if they had seen or heard anything.

According to Abbott, it would have been outside protocol for the state police to ask local police to canvas a neighborhood. He explains the reason the state police do it themselves is because they are trained in interviewing investigative techniques—how to be nonthreatening, to detect nonverbal cues, to listen, to know what to ask and when to follow up. There are positive interviews—where someone saw or heard something—and negative interviews where someone says they didn't hear or see anything. Both are important because down the line if the police find a discrepancy, they can go back to that witness and question them further.

Suspicions

It seems, according to their actions, that authorities had Peter Milliken in their minds as the prime suspect from almost the get-go. That afternoon, police began a multiday search of Peter's house. Of primary interest to investigators were why he had an arsenal of over thirty firearms in the second-floor semi-attic space. Peter says he was a gun collector. "They were looking maybe for a murder weapon or something like that because she was beaten with something," he explains.

If there had been evidence and Peter was involved, he's a smart guy and would have found a crafty way to dispose of it—not that he necessarily had to, considering authorities didn't look in the shed out back where Peter had an untagged deer hanging. "I'm not a game warden, that's not my job," is what one state detective told the neighbors when asked about this.

While the search of Peter's home was taking place, plainclothes detectives returned to the neighbor's home across the street. The neighbors aren't sure of certain details, as so much time has gone by and the experience was so traumatic things have blended together a bit. They do recall that it was cold and windy when the police returned, because they had a wood stove and the detectives warmed up by it. "It felt more temporary host than somebody who might be a source of information," the husband says. "Come in and get warm and how's it going."

At some point, the detectives asked the neighbors about their two cars. The husband used one, the wife the other. A detective inquired whether they left their keys in the ignition. Yes, they sometimes did. Would it be possible for Peter to have driven the car without them knowing about it? Unlikely. The driveway was on a bit of a hill, so it would be remarkable if a person or even two people could push a car up it and onto the street. They'd have to start the car, and the husband was pretty sure he and his wife would have heard that.

THE POSTMORTEM

Dr. Henry Ryan was the chief medical examiner for the state of Maine between 1976 and 1998. Prior to his appointment, the state relied on a coroner system. Larger towns might have had pathologists with some experience examining decedents. In rural areas, the person was often an older doctor who was semi-retired, maybe having sold their practice, and this was a way to make a little money. The problem, according to Lyndon Abbott, was a lot of the rural doctors took the word of whichever officer was on scene and wrote it off.

"Murder Most Foul"

During Ryan's tenure, the Maine medical examiner system developed into a centralized, modern organization. State statutes were updated. Educational programs were instituted, including one with the New England Seminar in Forensic Sciences at Colby College. Collaborative relationships with local and state law enforcement and the state crime lab were strengthened. A telephone system tied directly to the office was introduced.

Dr. Ryan wanted to be a teaching priest. He had a gift for the gab. He alternated between smoking a cigar and a pipe on scenes. He was meticulous and ethical. He was a philosopher and a storyteller who at crime scenes would quote from William Shakespeare's *Hamlet* the line "Murder most foul." He enjoyed simple pleasures like tuna fish sandwiches and a homemade dinner with colleagues. He was a New York City–raised devout Irish Catholic, a graduate of Manhattan College and the New York University School of Medicine. One of his all-time favorite things to do was watch birds. He even traveled with his brother out to the West Coast to go birdwatching.

At 2:30 p.m. that Saturday, November 6, Dr. Ryan was at Augusta General Hospital in the small morgue in the basement conveniently located just outside the loading dock. There were metal shelves lined up against one wall with labeled specimen jars. A scale, like the kind the butcher might use in a country market, hung from a metal hook. A stainless-steel table had a hole at the end located over the sink for convenient drainage.

This was Dr. Ryan's realm from 1976 till 1992 and the smell of his cigar hung in the room. The state created a permanent base for the Office of Chief Medical Examiner on the same Hospital Street campus in Augusta as the state police and state's crime laboratory in 1992, and Dr. Ryan worked there until he retired.

See for Oneself

Autopsies have been carried out at least since the days of ancient Greece. During the Middle Ages, they became an important source of information when investigating a murder. By the twentieth century, they were used to study diseases.

It was not uncommon for Dr. Ryan to do an autopsy the same day or even—as it was that weekend—two the same day. He preferred to do an autopsy as quickly as possible, feeling the best information was found as close to term of death.

In addition to Dr. Ryan, his assistant, the DA, Peter McCarthy and ideally both Willard Parker and James Pinette were in attendance. McCarthy would have been there primarily to collect fingernail clippings and hairs and fibers found on Dorothy's body by Dr. Ryan. These would go back to the lab for testing and then storage.

During the 1970s, there was not a lot of control of environment. State police would stand in the back. On at least one occasion, detectives brought in pizzas or sandwiches and stood in the back while the autopsy was being conducted.

An autopsy usually takes two to three hours, but depending on the number of injuries, they can take five or six.

A Careful Autopsy

Dr. Ryan wore worn pink rubber gloves and a green scrub top during the surgical portion of Dorothy's autopsy; however, he might not have during the preliminary examination. Forensic DNA was not part of the landscape yet, and the idea of contamination thus not considered.

Dorothy's body lay on the table cocooned in a nonporous vinyl or heavy-duty plastic body bag. Dr. Ryan, or his assistant, would have taken a picture of the body bag and then opened it and taken another photo to document how Dorothy's body arrived at the morgue. Her hands would then have been photographed and nails clipped. Dorothy's body would have been photographed with clothing on and then the garments handed to McCarthy to put into evidence. Dr. Ryan would've tried to remove her clothing without cutting it to preserve it as it was. Once her top, jeans and underwear were removed, he and his assistant would have turned Dorothy over to look at her back. Then her body would have been washed so they could really see any injuries. More photos would have been taken. Any pattern injuries (made by a blunt instrument) would have been measured and documented. Parts of her body that were not injured would also have been photographed to show the normal body that's there. The last nonsurgical step would have been for Dr. Ryan to draw a diagram of Dorothy's injuries, including measurements.

Very much like a surgical procedure, Dr. Ryan would have then made a Y-shaped incision that came down diagonally from each shoulder and curved slightly around each breast before reaching the middle of the body, and then continuing down to her pubis. He would have then examined Dorothy's chest, abdomen and cranial cavity. During this process, he would have taken samples from all her organs, put those in bags, and given them to his assistant, who would bring them back to Dr. Ryan's office for storage or processing into microscopic slides. It's possible the assistant also brought the blood to the lab for testing. McCarthy would have taken the evidence back to the crime lab.

Every detail of Dorothy's young body would have been described in detail. The weight of individual organs, the contents of her stomach, every bruise. The scar on one of her hands from when she got it caught in the pulley in the barn and got a rope burn.

Finally, he would have sewn Dorothy's body up. That evening or within the next day or two, Crosman Funeral Home in Lisbon Falls would have picked it up.

Dr. Ryan's report confirmed she died from a fractured skull sustained in the beating.

THE OTHER MURDERS

The headlines of the November 6, 1976 edition of the *Lewiston Evening Journal* read:

"Sabattus Mother Is Found Slain in Lewiston"
"Police Probe Slaying at the Fairgrounds"
"Body Is Found in Horse Barn"
"Body Discovered at Laundromat"

Seven hours after the Lewiston police received a call about Dorothy's body and only three after McBride's, DA Delahanty stated there was, as of yet, no reason to assume there was a link between the two murders. "There doesn't seem to be any apparent connection at this time," he said. He declared this when it was still being reported there were no suspects and no motive had been determined and in a town where it would, law enforcement believed, be the first day they could remember that there were two unrelated killings in a single day.

While people were ensconced in their homes reading about the tragic events of the weekend, Lewiston police were packing up the barricades and opening up Dorothy's crime scene. According to Abbott, it absolutely should not have been released for at least another day or two. Whether it was because the owners had gone to the mayor's office or the local chief of police lobbying to reopen their business, state police realized it had already been contaminated and there was nothing more there or detectives assumed it was Peter and were focusing elsewhere, who knows.

The Next Day

That weekend, crews from the Lewiston Public Works Department flushed the catch basins in the vicinity of the laundromat in search for a weapon. The theory was the weapon could have been passed through the grates of a nearby manhole. They didn't find anything. The weapon from Dorothy's murder has never been located.

Over the next few days, detectives interviewed Gerald, Peter, Gail, Dorothy's coworkers and certain members of her family. Several individuals said the police didn't ask pointed questions. They seemed more concerned with putting people at ease. They didn't ask if anyone knew of someone with a grudge against Dorothy or if she'd complained about anyone or seemed scared or worried.

Several close friends of Dorothy's who'd known her since 1968 or 1969 and lived in Lisbon or Lewiston at the time were interviewed by the state police shortly after Dorothy's murder. They were asked when the last time they'd seen Dorothy was. At least a couple had seen her that Thursday or Friday when they dropped off money for the Beeline Fashions home show at her house. One recalled seeing bags of laundry in the shed. They were also asked who they thought it could have been—if Dorothy was afraid of anyone. They told the police Dorothy hated a man by the name of Lionel Lussier and that he hated her. According to one of her friends, the group used to go the Heathwood Inn in Lisbon on Friday nights. The friends knew of at least two occasions when they were there and Lussier had words with Dorothy. One friend describes him as a mean drunk.

Arrests

At around seven o'clock Sunday evening in North Jay, another old mill town about thirty-four miles as the crow flies from Lewiston, Georgia Smith, forty, shot Michael Turmenne, twenty-seven, in her home. Turmenne had been a resident of the Auburn YMCA. The incident was reported minutes later, and State Trooper Alfred Hensbee arrested Smith at approximately eight o'clock that night.

A couple of hours later, a twenty-year-old Lewiston man named Scott B. Snow was arrested for the murder of the sixty-nine-year-old stable hand

Robert "Shorty" McBride. A newspaper photograph of Snow showed him to be tall and thin, with shoulder-length dark hair, wearing a red plaid flannel shirt and faded jeans, walking with an air of confidence. He was booked at the Lewiston Police Department and held without bail in the Androscoggin County Jail in Auburn. Later, he was briefly committed to the Augusta Mental Health Institute for an examination. The next month, he was indicted for first-degree homicide. In court in April 1977, he was found guilty, and the judge sent him to Maine State Prison for life. He was released in 1985.

Publicly at least, Snow has never been described by authorities as a suspect in Dorothy's murder.

STAKEOUT AND ANTIQUE THEFT RING

One theory Tonia and Mary Ellen have regarding Dorothy's murder is that she knew people involved in a multistate breaking-and-entering ring that was active in the area in 1976 and that she was going to go to the police with information. Dorothy was very protective of her family, and the thinking goes that if she believed Peter was somehow involved and got arrested that would not only take away the primary breadwinner but also potentially put her children in danger. If she felt she could preempt that or stop the theft ring, maybe things would be safer.

No one spoken to for this book actually heard Dorothy say she had a meeting set up with the Lewiston police. Interviews indicate rather that for years, Dorothy had remained silent about illegal activities she knew people close to her were involved in. Why all of a sudden would she go to the police?

Two former homicide detectives, neither of whom worked on Dorothy's case or the theft ring investigation, don't buy it. They believe that if she had been planning on going to the cops with information she would've been threatened before being killed. If she was going to be killed for going to the police, she would more likely have been shot in a far less visible spot than beaten to death in a public one.

Years after Dorothy's murder, her friend Glenda was working at Bath Iron Works and asked a former Auburn police officer working security there if he knew anything. He said, "She should have kept her mouth shut." Glenda doesn't know about what and isn't 100 percent sure he wasn't just being protective and warning her not to pursue the matter in general.

Stakeout

For three or four nights in the early days of the investigation, Lewiston officers, as requested by the state police, watched a potential suspect's home in Lisbon. A former cop who participated in the stakeout says it was a guy with a record who hung around with a few people who also had records.

It's possible the homeowner being watched was Lionel Lussier. A twenty-eight-year-old man with a record of multiple assault charges, he lived in Lisbon at the time. He was friends with Peter, and a couple years before Dorothy was killed, he got into a physical altercation with her. The story goes, depending on who you talk to, that Dorothy said something he didn't like—or it might have been he said something she didn't like—and angry words and yelling ensued. Lussier grabbed the hair wig she was wearing and her purse and threw them outside. Another time, a friend of Dorothy's recalls Lussier saying to her, "If you throw that at me, I'll hit you just like I hit a man." She didn't throw the drink at him, but her friend said she sure wanted to.

When asked directly for this book who he thought might have killed his wife, Peter offered up Lussier. Whether he did to police back in 1976 is unknown. And did he really believe this, or was he trying to divert attention away from himself or someone else?

About a month before Dorothy's murder, Lussier was charged with aggravated assault. Police allege that he followed a car carrying five sailors from the nearby Brunswick Naval Air Base and repeatedly attempted to run the car off the road by striking it several times over a span of several miles. *Of note, the same day Lussier was indicted, so was a man by the name of Michael Boucher. Boucher was charged with using a knife to cause injury to a woman in Lewiston. In 1991, after investigators uncovered new evidence, Boucher would be convicted of beating and strangling to death an eighteen-year-old girl who looked remarkably like Dorothy on September 15, 1973, in the nearby town of Litchfield. The girl's boyfriend was a Lewiston police officer at the time and was working on his car at Healy's Garage diagonally across from the laundromat when Dorothy was murdered. Boucher died in prison in 2022.

In May 1979, Lussier became the twenty-first person convicted in a two-year federal probe of antique thefts centered in Maine. He received an eight-and-a-half-year sentence for seven counts of burglary, theft and receiving stolen goods and one count of arson.

The antique theft ring involved dozens of persons operating in northern New England stretching through eight counties of Maine with stolen goods transported into New Hampshire, Vermont, Massachusetts and New York for sale. More than $100,000 ($433,603 in 2024) worth of bronze statues, antique chairs and brass beds, clocks, glassware, art and china was recovered from robberies of homes and businesses. It was described by a Massachusetts state trooper as a stolen antiques ring that operated "by contract."

By June 1985, Lussier was back on the street and arrested for operating under the influence. Police alleged he became violent and had to be restrained and was subsequently charged with a possession of a firearm. A few months later in November 1985, Lussier was acquitted in Androscoggin County Superior Court of an aggravated assault charge. He denied hitting a woman with a chair, a beer bottle and his fists when a fight broke out at a social club in Lewiston.

Between 1990 and 1994, he accumulated a number of misdemeanor charges. In December 1994, he was sentenced by a U.S. District Court to pay restitution of $966 and received a thirty-one-and-a-half-year prison sentence plus five years of supervised release for possession of a firearm by a convicted felon, using a firearm during a drug-trafficking crime and conspiring to possess marijuana with intent to distribute. He and three other men had broken into the wrong house looking for drugs and held a man at gunpoint.

During Lussier's 1994 trial, Tonia went to the courthouse and made eye contact with the man. She says she looked like her mom at the time and was trying to get under his skin. Tonia wanted to see if she could provoke a reaction that might tell her if Lussier had anything to do with her mother's death. She did not get anything.

Prior to his trial, one of Dorothy's friends was at a club in Lewiston with her husband, and they ran into Lussier. She describes him as having been drunk at the time and crying and telling them he did not kill Dorothy. He said he knew they all thought he did but that he didn't.

A lifelong friend of Lussier's who spent time in jail for theft and drugs told Tonia he didn't believe Lussier was involved in her mother's murder. While he communicated that he knew Lussier had a reputation for fights and trouble, he never got the impression he hated Dorothy. Supposedly though not considered a suspect himself, the man was polygraphed in or around 1978 and asked if he knew anything about Dorothy's murder. He did not. This man was involved in the aforementioned stolen antiques ring.

According to an article by longtime crime reporter Mark LaFlamme in the February 19, 2001 edition of the *Sun Journal*, Lussier was interviewed by another *Sun Journal* reporter in 1995 while he was in a federal prison in Pennsylvania. Lussier denied any involvement in Dorothy's death.

WELCOME TO LEWISTON

Arriving in Lewiston, the dramatic spectacle of a 250-foot-tall brick smokestack reminds visitors this town was once the blue-collar metropolis of Maine. Located thirty-six miles from Portland and a little over thirty-three miles from the state's capital, Augusta, Lewiston was struggling to remain relevant in 1976.

Twenty years earlier, everywhere you looked there was a success story. The textile mills were turning out millions of yards of cotton goods, while across the river in Auburn, the town's shoe industry was producing tens of thousands of shoes weekly and its brickyards supplying bricks for company housing and regional communities. The sidewalks were loaded with people shopping for everything from dresses and furniture to tea and toys in family-owned shops. Theatergoers enjoyed the likes of showman William "Buffalo Bill" Cody and screen legend Marlene Dietrich. The Grand Trunk Railroad Station, known as "The Depot" for Lewiston and Auburn, welcomed thousands of French Canadian immigrants.

By the 1970s, however, the area's industrial future was in deep trouble. The Great Depression, World War II, labor issues and lack of technological advancements all contributed to the gradual decline of the area's economy. When the factories closed, husbands commuted to mills farther out and wives took retail jobs at stores in the local mall or became secretaries for companies lured to the area. In many cases, people who could not find other jobs left. The population fell from around sixty-four thousand in 1950 to nearly forty-two thousand in 1970.

Law and Order

At times it must be remarkable, absurd and hair-raising what a police officer walking their beat sees on a daily basis. For former Lewiston mayor Larry Gilbert, who was a patrol officer with the Lewiston police between 1969 and 1974, it was walking some inebriated soul into the station to get booked while community members sat in folding chairs watching—bags of popcorn in hand.

Gilbert and his fellow officers had their own front-row seats to what was referred to by locals as an "adult entertainment area" composed of several blocks that once housed charming family-owned department stores, bakeries, grocers and lunch counters. Bars grew up on seemingly every corner; there were drugs and prostitution. People were passed out on streets. There were street fights. And live music flowed out of nightclubs and restaurants all over town—The Warehouse, 17 Park, The Royal, to name a few.

Police headquarters was located on the first floor of city hall on Park Street from the 1930s to 1986. The station was cramped, with crumbling, windowless offices. The locks on holding cells were weak, and the jail was described as dirty, smelly and—at one point back in the late thirties—filled with vermin. The dispatch center, which also served as a records department and traffic bureau, sat just off the unheated garage. A polygraph was procured in 1973, but it's unclear where that sat and whether anyone was trained to use it. Federal money funded miscellaneous technical equipment for the detective bureau in 1975. Until they moved into their new digs, the police did not have fingerprinting or darkroom equipment and all evidence had to be sent to the state police, the FBI and the Department of Human Services.

During the 1970s, women were relegated to secretarial roles. Industrial steel desks were covered with thick files, stacks of paper and overflowing inboxes. Clipboards and massive corkboards hung on or were propped up against walls. Detectives, young uniformed patrol officers and officials buzzed about smoke-filled rooms.

Lewiston's Own Boss Hogg

"Younger Longtin Injured While Cleaning Shotgun" declared the *Lewiston Daily Sun* on December 20, 1976. Longtin's twenty-seven-year-old son

Maurice, who lived in Sabattus, suffered an accidentally self-inflicted gunshot wound from a .410 shotgun. After being wounded, he called his father, and an ambulance quietly took him to hospital. Androscoggin County Chief Lionel Cote defended Longtin's son saying that because of a number of burglaries in the area, he normally kept the weapon loaded in his home. The incident happened on Saturday afternoon and was not reported to the public until Monday.

In 1979, Longtin was accused of shelving cases that involved VIPs. In 1980, he opposed city planners' application for a federal grant for $27,745 that would fund a crime analyst who would collect crime statistics and keep police departments informed on countywide burglaries. The program was supported by five of the county's seven police departments. Longtin had what was described in the February 1, 1980 edition of the *Sun Journal* as "serious reservations about the program"—he was supposedly afraid his officers would quit and refused to assign one of his officers to a proposed burglary task force.

Longtin has been described by former officers as having long been removed from actual policing and detective work. He was largely bound to his office unless a high-profile opportunity arose that drew him out—such as the brutal murder of a young woman.

On the Beat

Until the 1980s, the police had four or five people on foot beats. These were generally individuals in their first months on the job with the least amount of training. One former police detective said these beats were great connectors for the police because patrolmen got to know everybody on the street. However, he explained, that closeness between the police and the neighborhood community could lend itself to corruption. You've got a coffee shop and a police officer has been walking around all night. He's freezing his ass off, and some guy says, "Come on in. I'll give you free coffee." And you're not just giving him free coffee to be nice. In Lewiston, the boys in blue were at the very least enjoying complimentary newspapers and free coffee and the occasional hot donut fresh off the conveyor belt of a local donut chain.

Once in a while, a young officer on a foot beat would get picked up or ride along with a seasoned officer in a car. For rookies, this was a prime learning opportunity and one some took advantage of as much as possible before going to the twelve-week basic police school at the end of their first year.

"You learned a lot from the cruiser people," a former Lewiston officer explains. "So much so that I rode around on my days off with cruiser people just to try to learn the job. I felt so unprepared untrained and what do I do. If you smell pot coming out of a door, what can you do? At the time, pot was a big thing. Can you arrest them? How does this all work? I wanted to be able to do it."

New recruits also had a week of in-house training that included watching police training films and one afternoon of shooting their .38 Smith & Wesson revolvers into a local sand pit.

"I couldn't even buy bullets for my gun at age twenty," a former Lewiston police officer shares. "I was too young. I went to go get some time to practice at the range, and they said, 'No we can't sell those to you, you're too young.' I said, 'Well, I could be the guy who comes to your robbery tonight.' They sent an older policeman to illegally buy my bullets."

Misconduct

Mac Herrling spent the summer of 1972 working with the Lewiston police as a trainee. He says there was a perceived emphasis on property crimes and keeping the guys at The Manoir (a sketchy dive bar where sex workers were known to hang out) in their place by smacking them around if they got too drunk and disrupted the neighborhood. "We ignored prostitution being transacted at the bus terminal or on the street corner," he adds.

Mac says some officers were lenient with known prostitutes in exchange for sexual favors. It's unclear how widespread this practice was, how informed upper management was and if there was any disciplining.

"I found a new girlfriend by looking up her registration plate on the system after she droves 'round and 'round my downtown beat," Mac shares. "It was standard practice."

When the author inquired about police behavior during the 1970s, there were multiple insinuations that police officers took bribes to overlook high-stakes poker games at lock and key social clubs. These claims could not be confirmed.

FUNERAL RITES

On November 12, a week after Dorothy's murder, mourners gathered at West Bowdoin Baptist Church to pay their last respects. The copper-colored casket Peggy had picked out stood in the front of the packed sanctuary. "How Great Thou Art" played on the organ.

Sprinkled in among family and friends were plainclothes detectives—at least that's what family members assume, as they remember seeing a few people they did not recognize.

RONALDO AND LOIS PAID for the funeral and decided to have an open casket. Considering the extent of Dorothy's facial injuries, this decision surprised a few people. But perhaps this was simply an opportunity for them to see her one last time and let her loved ones say goodbye. Open caskets, Bob says, were also common then.

Peggy went into the funeral parlor early so she could see her sister and say goodbye. "I can remember standing at that door to go in, and I said, 'God you got to help me with this because this is the hardest thing I'd ever done in my life,'" Peggy shares. "I remember going in and looking at her, and it kind of looked like her but it didn't and touching her and all of a sudden—I don't know if you believe in things, but I do—all of a sudden, this calm came over me. I can't even explain because I was a wreck and touching her, and God said, 'You're OK, her soul is already with me.' I was so strong because my parents came in and my mother was so upset and Mary came in and fell on the floor and started crying. I was able to say, 'Mama she's not there. She's in heaven. You don't need to worry anymore.' You cannot imagine—it was the weirdest thing. I'd never touched a dead person in my entire life, but I had to do this. I just had to. There was no choice."

As guests passed by the casket, they could not see the full extent of Dorothy's injuries because of the way the funeral director had positioned the casket.

Bob recalls the body in the casket didn't look like Dorothy. Her face was stitched and swollen. He explains he knew it was his sister, but it didn't feel like her. Bob says he wanted to remember Dorothy the way she was. "Her hands were broken," her friend Sue recalls.

> *I was pregnant. I stood in front of her casket looking down at her in a daze. I was just beginning to wear maternity clothes. Donna* [a friend] *made me go sit down. Tears were streaming down my face. She had a lot of makeup on her forehead. Her skin was bluish. I assume that's from the bruises. She still looked like Dotty. Her hands were linked together. I knew whoever did the work on her had to have done extensive work to have an open casket. Her forehead was sloped.*

A forensics expert not involved in the case explained that slope was likely because when there are multiple fractures, pieces don't fit back together into the rounded shape of the skull.

Dorothy was buried in West Bowdoin Cemetery. Past the low black wrought-iron gate and stone pillars down a dirt road surrounded by trees and pasture is her grave.

HER TOMBSTONE READS:

DOROTHY LR MILLIKEN
AMN US AIR FORCE VIETNAM
JULY 5, 1948   NOV 6 1976.

As the others filed out of the churchyard, Ronaldo didn't move. He would not leave until dirt covered her coffin. He alone started filling the grave.

Peggy explains his heart broke when Dorothy died. She remembers him sitting in the living room weeks or maybe months later under her and her sibling's framed high school graduation photos. Tears were streaming down his face. He told Peggy that you're never supposed to die before your children.

Peter says of that day that the funeral was "crazy" and that there were too many flowers. They were "hideous."

Gail Ann did not attend.

IT'S ALWAYS THE HUSBAND

In 1976, Peter Milliken was a physically fit twenty-seven-year-old who had dropped out of high school his junior year, did siding and roofing and occasionally helped out his brother—a long hauler based in northern Maine—with mechanical stuff.

He has been described as charming, a talented mechanical guy and a habitual liar. He can fix anything with his hands and a few basic tools. He lies unnecessarily and with absolute confidence. It's impossible to tell sometimes if he's telling the truth.

"Peter is somebody that has an extreme talent," one acquaintance shared. "He could look you right in the eye and say that he was giving you a piece of green cheese from the moon, and you'd probably believe it."

He has never been presented to the public as either a person of interest or a suspect in Dorothy's murder. He was given the polygraph twice and passed both times. However, in the early days at least, it's not hard to see why some members of law enforcement considered him a good suspect.

A few of Dorothy's friends and relatives have stated they wouldn't be surprised if it was him, but they also would not be surprised if it wasn't.

From a conversation held in 2024, retired state police detective Peter McCarthy, who was part of the initial investigation, was adamant Peter Milliken killed his wife. That Peter was an enraged, jealous husband. Family members, however, feel he was generally mentally abusive and negligent but not prone to jealousy.

It's not clear whether McCarthy ever spoke with members of Dorothy's family and got to know who she was—or, for that matter, who Peter was at that time. The police supposedly didn't ask family or friends if Dorothy had been cheating on Peter, but in interviews for this book, every single person who knew her said she was loyal. She would not have violated their marriage vows. Most also say Peter was suspected of stepping out with other women, including possibly Gail, while she was sleeping on their sofa.

McCarthy's former colleague Lyndon Abbott says, "If he thought something happened, if he thought the husband did it—like in the Milliken case—you couldn't sway him off of that if hell froze over."

> *Policemen go to the scene and decide what happens. You never, ever do that. You go to the scene, read it, do a scene investigation, do a neighborhood investigation, gather all the evidence you can find, treat it so it can be used years down the road, and then when it points to somebody you say OK maybe he's the one. But you don't do that at the scene because he's a bad guy who was in the area.*—Abbott

Did the investigators' presumption of Milliken's guilt prevent them from pursuing other leads to any serious extent?

When talking to Peter about Dorothy, her murder and the investigation, it's as if he is reading off a script that he wrote a long time ago—as if he's stuck on a verbal treadmill and can't get off but also isn't really making an effort to do so. And one can't help wonder, What does he know? Who is he protecting? Why won't he just be honest—lay down his cards—and help solve this case? After all these years. Decades. If he really loved Dorothy, wouldn't he want her murderer(s) brought to justice?

Most of the people spoken with for this book believe he did love her. They also believe he knows more than he's said about what happened—again, this could be relevant to the investigation or not. He might have not said anything initially because he was scared of something or someone. He could have been protecting someone he knew or thought was involved. Peter maintains that he was asleep and had no idea Dorothy left the house to go to the laundromat. That seems far-fetched—and according to Mary Ellen by way of Gail, not true—but it doesn't make him guilty of murder.

When police talked to Peter in the weeks following Dorothy's murder, he was seen as deceptive. A former homicide detective explained most people you talk to in the course of an investigation are not going to be truthful. But he says it's a question of why they're telling you a story. Sometimes it has nothing to do with the case.

Off-Script

When Peter talks about his childhood, it seems like an honest conversation. He opens up about growing up in the rural community of Durham, Tuesday night Boy Scout meetings, Thursday night youth fellowship at the church down the street from his home, a mild interest in baseball and a passion for hunting and fishing. He's always been into industrial arts (welding, woodworking, drafting, electrical) and automotive technology. Peter volunteers that he learned to swim in the pool at the YMCA in Auburn and became a certified lifeguard.

He says his stepfather ran a junkyard and that when there was nothing to do, he'd go there and take stuff apart just to see what it looked like on the inside. When Peter was twelve, his stepfather helped him take a motor out of a vehicle, and he put the car back together, taught himself to drive and drove that car through the field all summer.

He remembers his mother, Hilda, and stepfather divorcing. He quit high school his junior year because he figured he could make more money roofing and siding than the teachers made.

His mother said that his father had died when actually he was alive and lived in Maine and even knew Peter. This was something Peter found out only after his mother had died and he took a DNA test. He says he asked her about this on her deathbed and she lied to him even then.

Hellraiser

In 1967, at the age of seventeen, Peter started to accrue a list of misdemeanor offenses. Over the next two years, these included: driving an uninspected motor vehicle, speeding tickets, public intoxication and driving under the influence. He admits to years of alcohol abuse and drunk driving. His record is nothing to raise a warning flag on its own, but what people had to say about him, his lying, his fight with Dorothy earlier in the day before she died and his associations certainly made him a person warranting further attention by the police—at least at the time.

Dashboard Incident

Dorothy normally didn't talk about her relationship with Peter, but that summer of 1976, she shared with a friend and her brother Bob that Peter had gotten angry and punched a hole in the dashboard of their car. She wasn't nonchalant when retelling the incident, her friend says. She was concerned. It's not clear whether police knew about this incident, as they chose not to speak with Bob or ask her friend what she knew about Dorothy's marriage when interviewed.

Car in a Field

When talking to Peter that Sunday or Monday in early November 1976, authorities were trying to figure out whether or not Peter had transportation to Lewiston. He told the police he had nothing to drive. However, family and friends say Peter's friend Randy, who he was with earlier the day Dorothy was killed, was loyal and would have done anything for him—including, they insinuate, help him commit a crime and cover it up. When Tonia spoke with Randy in the 1990s, she says he was not forthcoming about anything to do with her mother. He died in September 2008, so no one can question him again.

Then there's this old unregistered car in a field Peter was working on a day or two after Dorothy's murder. It was jacked up on blocks, and the wheels had gone missing. Mary Ellen is sure the wheels were on that Friday and missing that Saturday. An acquaintance of Peter's says that with his skills, he could have had the wheels on and off in twenty minutes. The neighbors don't know about that car but do remember a homemade green skidder that was made out of an old car or truck with big tires that Peter could drive in the woods. Definitely not road ready, they say.

Presque Isle

Peter's older brother Dale lived in Presque Isle and drove long haul from the time he got out of the U.S. Army in 1972. He went all over the country, but his primary route was Maine to Indiana. Occasionally, Peter says, he would go on the road with him doing mechanical work on the truck. He went to Presque Isle on regular trips while married to Dorothy, and that is where he says he went to live after she was killed because his brother was there.

Not long after Dorothy was killed, maybe a month or so, Peter took Pete from Mary Ellen's home and Erica from Peggy and Moe's and brought them to Presque Isle. A former girlfriend of Dorothy's who he was already sleeping with took care of the children there for about nine months, by which time she'd had enough and called Peggy to come get the kids. Moe; Mary's husband, Glen; Peggy; and Tonia drove up to retrieve them. Moe had a gun in the glovebox, not knowing what Peter might do. Nothing happened. Peter gave the children over without a fight.

Dorothy's sisters later became legal guardians of her children.

Later

Years after Dorothy's murder, her old friend Glenda saw Peter at a party. He was drunk, so she thought she'd ask him face to face whether he killed Dorothy and see if she got an honest answer out of him. She said, "Did you kill Dotty?" and he responded, "No, but I know who did." Then he walked away.

Peter remarried in 1986. As regards his having been questioned repeatedly over the years—though not by the cold case unit detective who's been on Dorothy's case since at least 2012—he says authorities always ask him the same questions. That they always wanted to have a conviction and didn't care who it was. He doesn't mind them working on her case but wants to be left alone.

The Husband Did It?

The theory of Peter as the murderer doesn't entirely make sense. He had ample opportunities, so why choose such a visible spot? There are plenty of back roads in Maine, and if he was going to kill his wife, he could have faked a car crash or killed her and hidden her body in a heavily wooded area where it might not have been found. Also, he seems to be the kind of person who would not have involved anyone else. He wouldn't have wanted to owe anyone. And what was his motive? It is alarming he was allegedly heard threatening her the night before she died.

Some of Dorothy's family think she was going to leave him, but that's hearsay. According to interviews, she never actually said she was divorcing him. Even if she planned to leave him—and worse maybe for him—if she knew something about him or his friends, again there are back roads aplenty and other steps to take before doing something so drastic as bludgeoning a woman to death.

According to at least one of Dorothy's post–high school friends, they did not remember Peter ever being violent and never thought he killed Dorothy.

THE TROUBLED TEENAGER

Gail Ann Hinkley was only ever a "troubled teenager" in the press coverage surrounding Dorothy's murder. There were no details about the young woman who could have been one of the last people to see Dorothy alive.

Gail claimed she was in the house on Pleasant Ridge Road at the time Dorothy was fighting with Peter. The closest neighbors maintain they did not see or hear the couple fighting, so any argument would presumably have taken place inside the home. Whether she was in the house when Dorothy left is a question mark.

Her mother, Barbara Hinkley, was already living in Florida when Gail moved in with Peter and Dorothy. She thinks Gail moved in late that summer, possibly in early August. According to Barbara, nothing remarkable happened while Gail was living with them—at least not until the end.

Mary Ellen remembers stopping by to see her sister. She wasn't home, but Peter was, and Mary Ellen saw Gail standing in the living room in her underwear and a long T-shirt. "I didn't want to think the worst, but I wasn't stupid," says Mary Ellen.

Tonia recalls holding and feeding Gail's baby son, Jeremy. He would spit up on her, and Dorothy would get angry because she'd have to change her clothes.

Running

What remains interesting, primarily because there's so much unknown about what she might have seen or known or been involved with, is how Gail behaved that Saturday after Dorothy's body was found. She moved out that day or possibly the next. Barbara and Mary Ellen say Gail was terrified of something and got the heck out of there ASAP—possibly even out of Maine. Conflicting accounts place her in Massachusetts for a few months or even a year or two in the late 1970s.

That Gail just up and took off, "That's Gail," her mom says, before relaying all she knows about Gail's movements and goings-on since 1976.

Barbara describes her oldest daughter as a caring person, fun-loving, someone who liked to party—a girl who knew what she wanted and would go after it, a very smart girl. "If she hadn't gotten herself pregnant in school, she would have been valedictorian," Barbara says. "She was plain smart. Picked up on everything right away. She wanted to be a lawyer. She went as far to get a student loan to try and go to college."

She was living in Thornton, Colorado and then moved to Florida and stayed with her mother for two or three months. Hooked up with a guy she lived with in South Beach, left him and hooked up with another guy and the two of them bought a house in Dania Beach near Fort Lauderdale. By this time, she had two children: Jeremy and a younger girl whose name Barbara thinks was Crystal. Gail and her children lived in Dania Beach for a few years; then she split up with the guy and moved out. There was an issue about not making house payments.

The last Barbara heard from her daughter was when Gail was living in Mississippi. She called her mom from the bar where she was bartending and wanted her to ship her shotgun. She needed to sell it, she told her mom, to get $350. Barbara refused but said she'd send a check for $350.

That was in the 1990s. Barbara hopes she is still alive but wonders. "She was into drugs real bad and always partying," Barbara shares. "Whatever happened in Maine happened in Colorado too. I think she saw something go on there. When she got to Florida, it was a let's get the hell out of Dodge type thing. I think Gail Ann has always been a little on the shady side."

When Gail left Florida for Mississippi, she sent Jeremy to live with her brother David in Maine, and Crystal was sent to a friend in Illinois. As far as Barbara knows, Crystal is in Illinois, but she doesn't have a good phone number for her anymore. They used to call back and forth she says.

Jeremy graduated from high school and moved to Coral Springs, Florida, where he got a job as a telemarketer. He used to see his grandmother once or twice a month, and then all of a sudden, he stopped coming. Barbara called, and there was no answer. She has no idea where her daughter or grandchildren are or if they are alive.

In the 1990s, while Gail was living in Florida, Tonia spoke with her for a couple of minutes. That's the last contact Dorothy's family has had with her. It's believed a state detective reached out to her around that time as well.

THE MISSED WITNESS

Fast-forward eleven months after Dorothy's murder. Mary Ellen is still reeling from her sister's death. She's balancing her painful memories with everyday tasks like picking up supplies for a Halloween party at the church. She's gotten everything on her list and is backing her car out of the spot in the store parking lot when she nudges another car. It's just a scratch, but she's an honest person, so she goes back inside the store and asks the clerk to help her track down the owner of the car. Then she goes outside and waits. Up walks a woman who introduces herself as Dorothy Couture. The two women exchange information and get to talking. It turns out Couture had been driving by the laundromat around the time her sister was killed. Mary Ellen tries to remain calm to take in the information. Couture explains she was going to pick up her son, who had been arrested for marijuana possession earlier in the evening. As she passed the laundromat, something made her look, and she saw a tall, light-haired man and a shorter dark-haired man in the parking lot. Both were wearing flight jackets (or leather jackets, which at night might be mistaken for flight jackets). Both were popular during the 1970s, so this doesn't really help narrow things down. It's not a large parking lot, and it's right off the street, so even in the dark she should have had a pretty clear picture—especially given it was a full moon with nary a cloud in sight and the bright lights of the laundromat backlit the scene. Couture doesn't see anything that prompts her to think there is any trouble and she continues on. Around one hour later, after picking up her son, she passes back by the laundromat, and this time Couture sees what looks like the woman sitting on the ground up against the side of the building. The two men are gone.

Excited to have this information, Mary Ellen urgently and repeatedly tries unsuccessfully to get someone with the Lewiston police to listen to her. No one wanted to talk to her.

A former Lewiston officer says back then it would have been common for the officer to pass a caller on to the state police. It's also possible, though less likely, the officer would have dismissed the information altogether because it was the state's case. They handled homicides after all.

According to Mary Ellen, she later found out that Couture had a reputation as an alcoholic and thinks this is why she was not believed and/or followed up with at the time. Eventually, Mary Ellen was able to connect with a state detective who confirmed Couture had picked up her son that night. Mary Ellen cannot recall which police station the son was at.

Couture was interviewed by the state police in the 1980s. It's believed this is because Mary Ellen shared her conversation with Couture with Detective Bruce Rafnell, who by then had been in charge of the case for a number of years.

In the late 1990s, Tonia spoke with Dorothy Couture, and Couture told Tonia the same thing she'd told Mary Ellen. Couture also told Tonia she got annual calls for a while telling her to keep her mouth shut. Couture has since passed away.

ANOTHER WOMAN

Content warning: This section covers difficult topics, including violence and death.

At around 9:30 p.m. two days before Thanksgiving 1976, thirty-year-old Janet Baxter left her seven-year-old daughter in their trailer on Oak Street in Oakland, Maine, to pick up cough syrup at the A&P store in the JFK Plaza on Kennedy Memorial Drive in the neighboring town of Waterville. At 9:59 p.m., she left the store. That was the last time she was seen alive.

Approximately two hours later, Norridgewock Police Chief Leroy Jones was standing on Old River Road across from the Old Oak Cemetery checking out a 1974 Ford sedan that was perched on the bank of the Kennebec River. It was stuck on the foundation of a derelict house. The car's motor was running. Shortly Jones was joined by Somerset County Sheriff's Deputy James Flanagin. They assessed the situation, and after several minutes, Flanagin opened the trunk. Inside they found Baxter's partially clothed body. Most of her clothes were missing. The autopsy would later confirm she'd been sexually assaulted and shot twice, once in the head and once in the chest.

There was no indication Baxter had been robbed. The car, which belonged to her boyfriend, had been found about a thirty-minute drive from the A&P. She'd been a licensed practical nurse employed by Thayer Hospital and Maine Physical Therapy Clinic, both in Waterville. She was recently divorced.

This was about one hour north of Lewiston, where Dorothy had been killed eighteen days earlier.

Detective Lyndon Abbott was put in charge of the investigation with support from Detective Parker, who had been removed from Dorothy's case after one week. Unlike Dorothy's investigation, administrators with the state police chose to keep the lead investigator initially assigned on board for the duration of the investigation. Additionally, Baxter's case was in the news almost daily for months. Her parents, who've been described as "well-to-do," had political connections in the Augusta area. There was significant pressure to solve this case.

Origins of a Possible Serial Killer

Albert Cochran, a local man who'd been released from an Illinois prison in 1973 for killing his wife and three children, was an early suspect.

In 1963, in Joliet, Illinois, Cochran was a twenty-five-year-old department manager at a discount house. He had recently separated from his wife, who was raising their three young children in the duplex home they formerly shared. One night he went over to the duplex, argued with his wife and, according to him, fell asleep on the floor. He told authorities later that he was awakened by his wife's raucous laughing. He said she told him she'd killed the children and then "I choked her and choked her and choked her until she dropped." Police found the body of Mrs. Cochran wrapped in a blanket on the living room floor. Her neck had been broken. There was no blood found on her nightgown. A butcher knife lay on top of the children's bodies in the bathtub. Police retrieved the shirt and pants Cochran was wearing at the time of the murders and sent them to a crime lab in Chicago for analysis of some spots that looked like bloodstains. Cochran was only charged for killing his wife after the judge dropped the charges for murdering his children.

He passed the polygraph however many times he was given it but in September 1964 was sentenced to fifty to seventy-five years in prison with the option to apply for parole in eleven and a half years. He was released after nine.

According to Lyndon Abbott, there was a rumor that Cochran's mother had a lot of money and hired the best attorneys in Illinois. They petitioned annually for several years and finally convinced the judge to release Cochran to his mother under supervision on parole.

Coincidences

By 1976, Albert Cochran had relocated to Maine.

Abbott knew Baxter had been at the A&P store in JFK Plaza because her groceries were still in the car. When he interviewed people at the store, he found one witness who told him they saw someone in the car when Baxter got into it. Abbott says he knew she'd been alone when she got to the store, so the assumption was whoever was in the car was likely also responsible for kidnapping her. According to Abbott, no one has ever been able to confirm if Baxter drove at gunpoint or if her kidnapper drove her car.

It turned out that Cochran had left his car in the lot of the JFK Plaza and that he'd been seen by Skowhegan police walking toward Norridgewock, where his brother lived, from Skowhegan the night Baxter was killed. When Cochran was interviewed by police, he denied any involvement in Baxter's murder and said he'd been picked up in Waterville by three strangers. He jumped out of their car and was walking to his brother's, and that's why he was on the road. His brother, who ran the construction unit Cochran was working for at the time, backed him up, saying his brother had come to his house that night. But Cochran's story didn't sit right with Abbott. He couldn't, among other things, satisfactorily explain why he'd left his car in the lot in Waterville.

Abbott knew Cochran's history and that he'd been in the area when Baxter was killed. A warrant was obtained to compare Cochran's hairs with those found in Baxter's car. The test proved inconclusive.

Pauline Rourke

On December 15, 1976, Pauline Rourke disappeared. She had been living with her daughter and Cochran in a mobile home in Fairfield, Maine. Rourke was last seen by her daughter, who reported overhearing her mother and Cochran arguing the night before she disappeared. Rourke was scheduled to be interviewed by the state police regarding the Baxter investigation as a possible witness against Cochran.

Aside from notices the first week after she was reported missing, Rourke was not mentioned in the media again until 1998, when biological evidence collected from Baxter's murder scene and run through newly developed DNA technology led to Cochran's arrest in Florida.

In 1999, a tiny drop of Cochran's genetic profile, which had been stored in the State Crime Lab since Baxter's body was discovered in 1976, convinced a jury he was guilty of her murder. Cochran denied any knowledge of Rourke's disappearance. He died in prison in 2017. Her body has not been recovered.

According to Abbott, who firmly believes Cochran killed Rourke, authorities have had a lead on where her body has been buried for years, but the Attorney General's Office said in the 1970s they could not come up with the $40,000–$50,000 it would cost to excavate that area due to where the body could be located. When the area was scanned sometime after 1985, the image was also not conclusive.

If you have any information about Pauline Rourke, please contact: Maine State Police, Major Crimes Unit-Central, 36 Hospital Street | Augusta, ME, 04330 | (207) 624-7076 x9.

GROWING COLD

November turned to December with doors and windows adorned with twinkling lights, elementary school holiday performances, sprinkle sugar cookies and snowy fields. But for Dorothy's loved ones there was no joy.

Since November 13, a week after Dorothy's murder, there had been no press coverage. Then on December 8, as the case entered its second month, the Lewiston Police Department announced they were adding two detectives to the investigation. Detective Lieutenant Normand Poulin and Detective Laurent Gilbert joined Detective Sergeant Roger Bisson, Detective Roland Morin, Acting Detective Herbert Saucier and State Trooper Bruce Rafnell.

Detective Captain Robert Soucy told the *Lewiston Daily Sun* the detectives would spend "all their time on the Milliken case and will not become involved with other activities." He did not explain the decision or offer any updates.

Two months later, nothing had come of the additional manpower. There were no new leads. Assistant Attorney General Richard S. Cohen, a small mustachioed man working from his plant-filled corner office in the statehouse, could share only that the investigative team had shrunk by three and was being worked by State Detective Rafnell and two local cops. He described it as "an active and full investigation." "Once we get to the stage where everything is completely exhausted, we still will be keeping the case open." He offered no explanation as to what investigators would do with an active case with no leads and theoretically nothing more to check.

The article also mentions how Dorothy had been found a few hours before McBride, both of whom were fatally beaten, and how law enforcement officials had maintained throughout the investigation the two murders were not related. Cohen reaffirmed that, stating, "We have nothing concrete to show that they are connected." He also acknowledged the police had not made any major developments in the case.

Fear and Threats

On the one-year anniversary of Dorothy's murder, the laundromat was still open for business, and area residents were going about their lives. All the Lewiston police could say was that the investigation would remain open until it was solved. Detective Sergeant Marcel Belanger stated some members of the family had since moved from the area. That's not accurate, unless he was referring to Peter, who had temporarily relocated to the northern part of the state, and Gail, the latter of whom was not family.

In October 1978, Cohen announced an active lead was being pursued but said no arrests were expected immediately. It turns out this development was a new informant referred to as "he" by Detective Rafnell; when polygraphed in January 1979, this informant helped police eliminate one lead and advance another.

In late February 1979, Rafnell was looking into an account from Dorothy's friends that she may have been threatened shortly before being killed. "I've heard several reports of a similar nature, but we haven't been able to confirm them," Rafnell stated.

Several of her childhood friends and two adult friends were interviewed for this book, two of whom have been questioned by police. None knew anything about any threats. However, Dorothy had two other close friends from Lisbon, where she lived in a family-based apartment complex in the mid-1970s. It's possible one of them spoke with police and knew about the threats. They are unable to confirm, as they have passed away.

What Rafnell might have been referring to and could have gotten from case file notes or previous interviews with family members—though why he would say it was from friends is confusing—is that a couple days before she was killed, Dorothy came home to find a lit candle on the table in the kitchen. According to her siblings Mary Ellen and Bob and her daughter Tonia, she was really upset by this.

Mary Ellen, who was interviewed in late 1977 or early 1978 by state police, says Dorothy was scared of something. She recalls Dorothy telling her during the summer of 1976 that some of her bras had gone missing from a dresser drawer and that she'd come home one time to a knife sticking straight up in the kitchen sink. Bob didn't know about the bras or knife.

Dorothy and Peter often left the house unlocked, so it could have been anyone. When she told Bob about the candle, he says she was visibly upset. He suggested it was Peter, because he, Mary Ellen and Peggy thought Peter played mind games. Dorothy told him no, she'd been out with Peter, so it couldn't have been. Then he immediately thought of Peter's friend Randy, who was thought to be willing to do anything for him. According to Bob, Dorothy didn't disagree.

During 1976, Tonia remembers they had a training potty in the outhouse for her sister Erica. "At night I would use the training potty so I didn't have to go out to the shed," Tonia explains. "One night I remember trying to be a big girl—going to bed with a flashlight and saying, 'I am going to go to the outhouse.' I did , and when I came out, my mother was standing there with a shotgun. She was like, 'Oh my god you scared the shit out of me.' So, what was she scared of? That's a question I have—what was she scared of?"

Unverified Rumors

After Mary Ellen spoke with the state police, she sent them to Dorothy's friend Sue's apartment. Sue recalls the officer being in uniform and assumes he was with the state, not Lewiston police. Sue says he told her he wanted to know what kind of girl Dorothy was in high school and what kind of guys she dated. She told him about Terry. He wanted to know if she was a serious dater (Sue's words), and she told him Dorothy was a one-guy girl.

Sue doesn't recall the officer's name or the other questions he asked. She believes he was "poking and prodding" because he'd heard Dorothy was promiscuous, a side of Dorothy that Sue never knew existed at all. She says she'd heard rumors that Dorothy had an affair with a married guy but didn't know if that was true. The man she describes was married and has a documented history of complaints from women. Several of Dorothy's friends interviewed for his book also individually shared stories that this man flirted with them and described him as a woman chaser.

The rumor lacked verification, and Sue says it made no sense to her. "I took the rumor as garbage," she states. "You couldn't charm Dotty. She'd be too smart. That guy had a reputation."

Dorothy's older brother Bob thinks whoever started the rumors about her having an affair was jealous. "It wasn't in her," he shares. "She cared about her kids. She had a really rocky marriage. If she was running around, I would say so."

Lack of Progress and Contact

In March 1994, news articles appeared quoting retiring Lewiston Police Chief Laurent Gilbert citing his regret that the department was unable to solve Dorothy's case. Tonia and her family were shocked. They hadn't heard from investigators or read Dorothy's name in the news for years. Police still had no suspect, weapon or motive. Authorities were also not making public any additional details.

As a response to Gilbert's comments, Ronaldo told the Associated Press that he hadn't spoken to authorities in years but thinks about his daughter's murder just about every day. "It's pretty hard to forget," Ronaldo said. "In one way I am (hopeful) I guess. But I'd hate to stir all these things up again."

A little over a year and a half later, on Sunday, November 12, 1995, he passed away, nineteen years and a week after Dorothy.

3

UNSOLVED

THE ORIGINAL DETECTIVE

Lyndon Abbott is a state police legend, a gentle giant at six foot five who has towered above many suspects. He was with the state police from 1964 to 1985, ten years of which he was a member of the elite homicide squad. Abbott led or was part of fifty-six murder investigations. A number of those were violent crimes by strangers against women that took place around the time of Dorothy's murder. He knew the state detectives working her case.

Abbott was the state police's neighborhood investigation guy. That was his thing. He was the person you'd spill your secrets to. Easy to talk to, knew his way around a small town and was more professional, less intimidating. For the older cases like Dorothy's, there weren't traffic cameras, cellphones or Facebook pages. Facial recognition software would not be used by police departments until 2016. That's why what Abbott shares here, while true today, was especially relevant in the 1970s:

> *Why good detectives solve cases sometimes comes down to you have to give a shit.…. You have to get out and knock on doors. You have to get out and talk to people. Day and night, then you see all the different stuff that's in their neighborhood. Who's delivering at two o'clock in the morning. Who's going through. Who's doing this. I sat down with drunks and drank a beer with them and found out what they really knew about the guy down the street. I didn't go for thirty-five minutes into a neighborhood, I went for a week.*

Background

These days Abbott is less tough guy and more wicked good storyteller. Still, he doesn't mince words. An asshole is an asshole. It's easy to imagine him portrayed in a television procedural that would be a Maine-based version of acclaimed author Michael Connelly's work.

Abbott was born in the central Maine college town of Waterville. When he was six, his family moved to nearby Benton. The town made it into a national tabloid in 1970 when a family found a mummified human foot in a room they were renovating. Coincidentally, it was none other than Abbott who was the responding officer when the foot's presence was reported to the state police. He took the foot to Assistant State Pathologist Irving Goodof at Mid-Maine Medical Center in Waterville. Dr. Goodof's opinion was that it was a child's foot that had been surgically removed thirty or forty years earlier. There were not good records from that time, and it proved impossible for Abbott to figure out whose foot that might have been.

As a preteen and teenager, he worked at the local Texaco station. It was there he met a few troopers by gassing up their cars. That's how he says he got interested in law enforcement. When he graduated high school, he didn't take the basketball scholarship the University of Maine at Orono was offering. He said it wasn't much anyhow. He drove a snowplow and worked in an automotive store before being accepted into the state police. In March 1964, he attended the police academy.

Abbott spent most days on his own traveling the state's dark back roads. He would go into towns so small they didn't have a police force. "Rural people really enjoyed us," Abbott says. "Portland PD, Lewiston PD, Waterville PD, Augusta PD, Bangor PD they hated our guts because we came in and took over the case and that's where they got all the notoriety." He explains that because the state police were not tied to a specific town or county the way a local force or sheriff's office is, they could work statewide without the burden of small-town political commitments and biases.

In 1970, he was promoted to plainclothes detective. "All I did at the time was take the blue light off my cruiser," he explains.

On January 31, 1972, Abbott was called to help locate a missing ten-year-old girl who collected stamps and attended Girl Scouts meetings in the tiny farming town of St. Albans. The town has the unique claim to fame of having been the hometown of folk legend Yodelin' Slim Clark. It was a clear day with temperatures close to zero, and everyone was searching for the girl, who had been seen with a young man on his snowmobile earlier in the day.

Abbott ended up in his cruiser with an eighteen-year-old farmhand who was one of the girl's neighbors and the boy's father. Abbott realized right away the boy had a developmental disability—when later tested it was estimated he had an IQ of 76. When Abbott asked him if he'd seen the girl at first, he said he hadn't, but Abbott could see he was lying.

"I said to his father, who seemed to be OK, 'Because of what's going on here I've got to give your son what's called a Miranda Warning before I talk to him because I suspect that he knows more than he's telling me about [the girl],'" Abbott recalls.

> I was an hour and twenty-two minutes explaining the Miranda Warning to them. "I am a police officer. Do you understand that? You do not have to talk to me. I ask you a question you can say I don't want to answer that. That's a privilege do you understand that?" And we went through the whole Miranda that way, "Do you understand?" and I said, "Do you wish to talk to me?" and they said OK.

The boy admitted he had gone for a ride with the girl on his snowmobile but said she'd gotten off and went with a guy they'd met. Abbott didn't buy it but let him tell a story about how he came home and did his chores and so on. Meanwhile, the search party had found the girl tied to a tree, frozen.

"I said 'I absolutely don't believe you,'" Abbott shares. "'I think something happened and you panicked and you tied [the girl] to a tree,' and he started crying. His father said, 'You tell the trooper the truth,' and he did." After the boy's admission, he was placed under arrest.

Being Honest About Death

During his time as a detective, Abbott estimates he attended around one thousand autopsies. "You become very honest about death right off quick," he explains. "You realize how easy it is to die and how hard it is to live."

He says you cannot just start coming unglued when you see a young woman brutally killed.

You've got to say OK very pretty lady—she's dead and I'm going to get the son of a bitch that did it and let's go right now. Let's start digging. And that's what you did. You had to keep that kind of level. You couldn't let yourself get emotionally involved.

Abbott became emotional only once in an autopsy. It was in 1970, and a young boy about the same age as his son was lying on the table. They were about the same height and weight and sort of looked alike. "I got thinking that could be my son on the table, and Jesus the tears started flowing down," he shares. He had to have a colleague come in and stay with the doctor while he went outside and smoked a cigarette. "I got my shit together and went back in and I was fine," Abbott recalls. "That was the first and only time I ever got to the point where I let my emotions overtake me. You can't do it. You go down the tubes in a hurry. It kicks you out right there."

"The God Squad"

In 1973, he was assigned to the elite eight-member Criminal Investigation Bureau (CIB), which was a temporary result of the restructuring of the Bureau of Criminal Investigation. The CIB was known as "The God Squad" in a comical sense. "I never could figure out where they got that from, that we were almost untouchable, which was horse manure. We weren't," Abbott says. "The thing that really wound people up was when I had a problem, I could pick up the phone and call the AG. Not one of his people. I could call him and say, 'Sir I need this this this.' You got it. That was the kind of power if you want or persuasion if you want."

In the 1970s, when a homicide occurred, there would be a primary detective assigned—ideally someone from the CIB—and several detectives. They might come from all over the state to work the case initially.

Dorothy's Crime Scene

"The biggest thing was we never wanted to do was contaminate the scene," Abbott says. "That scene [referring to Dorothy's] had to be, I don't know for a fact, but had to be botched," he shares. "The detectives on scene that day had not gone through all the training yet." Abbott is referring to a two-week-long homicide course he and members of the CIB took at the University of Baltimore called the Frances Glessner Lee Seminar in Homicide Investigation. There they, according to Abbott, studied all or some of Lee's eighteen handcrafted dollhouse-sized scenes of unnatural death. Lee (1878–1962) was the first female police captain in the United States and is considered the "mother of forensic science."

"Starting around 1976, lieutenants and sergeants were going to the scene and deciding what happened," Abbott explains. "Before that we went to the scene and learned what happened. There's a hell of a difference."

THE UNSOLVED HOMICIDE UNIT

When a case reaches Maine's Unsolved Homicide Unit (UHU), it has a sort of end-of-the-line feel to it. Staffing shortages and prioritization of current/new cases are the more blaring issues. Also, detectives are often working with deficient or improperly handled evidence and lack of witnesses.

Meanwhile, the families suffer. Birthdays and holidays are marked with social media posts—the family has no answers for their loved one. The case changes hands again—many times, depending on how old the case is. Posters are tacked up. Parents pass. Psychics and maybe private investigators are contacted. Rewards are posted. Family members go on podcasts and on television. They grieve and hash out among themselves who could have done this on a cyclical basis. Their pain sharpening then dulling then sharpening then dulling with every hope, every diminished response.

There is no statute of limitations on murder in Maine. A case may remain open and unsolved until the murderer is captured and convicted or confirmed dead.

All the cases essentially begin the same way. The circumstances surrounding the way the individual was found caused suspicion. A detective was assigned. Evidence collected. An autopsy performed. A number of people interviewed. Days turned into months, which turned into years.

The Maine State Police and the Attorney General's Office say the case is open, and whether active or inactive, no specific details can be provided. The case "has been worked on" in recent months. Tips are appreciated.

According to unit head Lieutenant Thomas D. Pickering, when a case is pulled off the state police's Unsolved Homicide website, it doesn't necessarily mean it's closed. It could be open but inactive. Names, he says, are semiregularly pulled off the list. Before this happens, there is a thorough review of investigative materials by the AG's office based on state police recommendations. Then, if the AG's office determines to remove the name from the published list, the family's representative is made a part of the process.

As of January 4, 2025, there are seventy-one people on the state's list of active open unsolved homicide victims.

Maine's Oldest Cold Case

One Thursday morning, July 22, 1954, twelve-year-old Daniel Wood Jr. set out from his home in South Gray with his fishing rod to go fishing. He was 4'6" tall and wore blue jeans, a white T-shirt and glasses. There was nary a cloud in the sky, and the light wind carried the promise of adventure. However, only ten minutes later, he phoned home from a store in Gray and told his mom he was going to make house-to-house calls with a salesman in Lewiston—a town about eighteen miles away—and would be home before dark. His mother either told him not to go or cautioned him not to ride with strangers, and he told her not to worry. That was the last anyone heard from him. Daniel was last seen by a classmate who said she saw him riding with four other persons (a man, woman and two children) in "an old maroon auto with yellow number plates." At that time, yellow registration plates were sometimes seen on cars from the Canadian Province of Quebec. The classmate also said she knew Daniel well and that he would hitchhike to Gray to go fishing. Nine days later, after an exhaustive search, two fishermen pulled his nude, badly beaten body from the Little Androscoggin River in Auburn approximately fifteen miles from his home. A decade on, the Auburn police chief said he believed the boy was the victim of a convicted child murderer serving a life sentence in Michigan. The chief tried unsuccessfully to interview the convict in 1963. Forty years later, in 2003, a local man sent a rambling letter to lawmakers and members of the boy's family saying he was molested by a neighbor of the family and believed he was responsible for the unsolved murder. A detective was assigned to investigate. Nothing has appeared publicly regarding the case since then.

Caseload

For some there are more details:

JOYCE TANERILLO WAS FOUND dead in her car, which was parked outside her Front Street apartment in South Portland in 1974. The twenty-nine-year-old woman had been strangled. Tanerillo was last seen alive shortly after midnight Monday morning August 26 in an Old Orchard Beach establishment, about eight hours before her body was found. She and her husband had divorced the week prior.

The above was the story until 1989, when for the first time her family and ex-husband Sebato "Sonny" Tanerillo, who had a history of violence, discussed specific details leading to her death with Steve Campbell of the *Evening Express* paper. Sebato says he saw Joyce "by chance" in The Lighthouse bar in Old Orchard Beach, where she was having a conversation with the bartender. Sebato describes having a few beers with Joyce, and a few minutes after midnight she agreed to have coffee with him at the Dunkin' Donuts in the Thornton Heights area of South Portland. The bartender walked Joyce to her car and told an Old Orchard Beach police officer walking by the bar that there might be trouble because Joyce and Sebato were arguing. The officer watched Joyce's car leave the lot, with Sebato's car following close behind. That's the last time Joyce was seen alive. Sebato says he followed Joyce to the nearby restaurant Clambake at Pine Point, where, according to him, she pulled over and picked up a young woman who was hitchhiking. He followed Joyce into Portland, where she dropped the passenger off, and then he lost her at a red light. He then went to the Dunkin' Donuts, where Joyce was a no-show. A neighbor of Sebato's told police he saw him drive up around 1:30 a.m. The article also quotes Sebato saying he became a prime suspect and that he and Joyce and "fought like cats and dogs." Tanerillo remarried in 1974 and died in 2020.

THE BODY OF TWENTY-EIGHT-YEAR-OLD **KENNETH KRAMER**, a merchant seaman and member of the rock band Country Fry, was discovered four miles from his home in the snow in front of an abandoned shack at the bottom of a small mountain. The isolated cabin stood along Route 182, a two-lane state highway that runs between the tiny towns of Cherryfield and Franklin in blueberry country. The area is known by locals to be haunted. The state's assistant attorney general described the murder victim as "an informant for police" and said police were looking into the possibility of that being related to his death. It is believed he was chased up the road a short distance before being shot and was shot again after he had fallen. That was in February 1983.

For some there are less:

Sean Conway left Robert Sanborn's motorcycle shop in the tiny town of Cornish, Maine, in York County one Wednesday evening in January 1991 and his body was found dumped on the side of the road near a cemetery a week later. His wallet was missing. He appeared to have been beaten.

In 1994, Raynald Levesque, the fifty-five-year-old operator of a bottle redemption center in a building behind his residence, was shot to death in his home three days after Easter in the small, working-class town of Madison in Central Maine.

Why Do Cases Go Cold?

There are homicide detectives who don't sleep, eat poorly, have a condition known as post-traumatic stress disorder and suffer burnout. They cruise through marriages, are distanced from their own children and hurt in ways no one who is not part of their world could truly understand. Their dreams the stuff of nightmares, their days spent chasing shadows.

So, with all these hardworking, dedicated souls, why do presumably solvable cases like Dorothy's go cold? It could be any number of reasons: mistakes in the investigation, contaminated evidence and issues with chain of custody, lack of witnesses, deaths of suspects, deaths of witnesses, a witness who recants their statement, inexperienced and/or incompetent investigators, an arrogant "law and order" mentality, leads ignored, alternative suspects not thoroughly vetted, interagency conflicts, lack of working equipment or limited resources. Interviewees lie, witnesses don't come forward, assumptions are made and on and on.

These are the cases that keep good detectives up at night: when there is a hypothetically strong suspect in a case, where there are plenty of facts that would support criminal charges but also mitigating factors that would prevent the attorney general from bringing the case forward.

One former homicide detective stressed how tunnel vision can be devastating to a case. Having a suspect is one thing; having them guilty is another. If you're only looking in one direction in any day of your life, what have you missed while you're not looking around? You see what you see, but you're oblivious to everything else happening around you. Is that what investigators did with Dorothy's case? Were they so focused on Peter Milliken they ignored everyone and everything that did not point in his direction?

It's been suggested cold cases are solved when relationships change—maybe someone dies or divorces—something prompts them to feel free of obligation. Also, deathbed confessions and developing forensics help.

How do detectives work cold cases? What is there to do on a weekly or even monthly basis after a decade or two or three or more? In 1995, Assistant Attorney General Tom Goodwin referred to Dorothy's case as active, as in "it's an open case with a detective assigned to it but not active in the sense that there's a lot of activity. It's been reviewed on a regular basis over the past few years."

Series of Detectives

Through the decades, Dorothy's case had been passed on from detective to detective as individuals retire and are promoted or transferred. Timothy Culbert had the case in the early and/or mid-1990s, possibly beginning in the 1980s. When he retired in 1998, the case was reassigned to Richard Fowler, who had it for several years. In the early 2000s, it was reassigned to Scott Gosselin. Detective Corporal Michael Chavez has had Dorothy's case since 2012, when he was promoted to detective in the Major Crimes Unit (MCU). In 2014, Chavez became assistant commander of the state's Underwater Recovery Team but held onto the case.

Detective Assigned

The following is a segment of my email interview with Chavez from May 2024, interspersed with notes about cold case procedure in Maine and Dorothy's case in particular. Neither the questions nor answers have been edited.

Q: At any given time, what is the average number of cases a member of the unsolved unit is actively working? Or if easier—the average number of open cases a detective has and whether that is a combination of active and cold.

A: There's no set number since all of our unsolved cases are still active and worked whenever new information comes in and at the discretion of the primary investigator. The UHU, at the moment, does not assume primary status on any unsolved case and work alongside each primary that was assigned to the case. There are currently over 70 unsolved homicides that span the years, along with over 30 suspicious missing persons cases that are worked by each primary. In the year that I've been working unsolved cases, I've dug into over ten cases so far, not including the ones that I had been assigned as a detective in MCU.

Q: Do members of the unsolved unit also work on active cases?

A: Right now, it's just me in the unit and yes, I still have active cases that I had been working on prior to joining the unit. The other detectives will be in the same boat. Additionally, we're in an on-call status within the Major Crimes Units every couple of weeks and will help investigate cases during that timeframe, should any come in.

> In 2015, when the Maine legislature approved funding for the UHU, it was created for the purpose of investigating unsolved homicides. The proposed unit would be staffed by a prosecutor and a victim witness advocate from the Attorney General's Office, a lieutenant and two detectives from the state police and a forensic chemist from the state's crime lab.
>
> On hearing from Detective Chavez that he was the only detective in the unit and was working active and cold cases, I wrote to the AG's office for more information. I relayed in an email in June 2024 that it was my understanding the UHU was understaffed and that staff were not dedicated 100 percent of the time to cold cases. The AG referred me to

Lieutenant Pickering, who, in addition to managing the UHU, is also in charge of Special Projects.

Following is a description of Lieutenant Pickering's duties as Head of Special Projects from a Facebook post published on August 25, 2022, announcing his promotion:

Some of the Special Projects Lt. Pickering will be working on will include enhancement, improvement or augmentation of technology and equipment used in law enforcement operations or adjustment of agency practices, processes and procedures. Other special projects may also include special initiatives as legislative work, initiatives originating out of the State Legislature, testimony and/or impromptu research or administrative tasks as identified by Central Command.

In June 2024, Lieutenant Pickering responded to my query regarding the staffing of the UHU. He wrote:

Currently there is 1 MSP Lieutenant, 1 Detective Sergeant, 1 Detective Corporal, 1 Detective, 1 Forensic Chemist II, 1 Criminal Intelligence Analyst, 1 Assistant Attorney General and 1 AG Victim Witness Advocate assigned to the Unsolved Homicide Unit. Some of these positions have been newly created or recently filled.

Those assigned to the UHU primarily work on unsolved homicides and suspicious missing persons cases. All the members assigned to UHU will support the Major Crimes Units as needed and are a part of an on-call rotation with all other state police detectives for "non-business" hours calls and weekends. The frequency of the on-call weeks are typically every 5 weeks, but frequency is resource driven. During a detectives on-call weeks they would be working with UHU unless they were called to assist. For example: A detective works Monday through Friday on UHU cases and gets called on Saturday for a suspicious death. The UHU detective would respond and assist with the investigation. As a need requires a UHU detective could be a primary on a current case, but this would be an exception and not a rule.

Q: What year did the Dorothy Milliken case move from active to unsolved?

A: The current guideline is that any homicide that remains unsolved after 3 years is considered an unsolved homicide. Dorothy's case has been actively worked since its occurrence.

Q: When was the last lead/development?

> During the course of my research, I found no indication that any member of law enforcement has spoken with members of Dorothy's family—with the exception of her daughter Tonia—friends, associates or former neighbors in the past decade regarding the case. Most have not been contacted since the 1970s, if ever.
>
> When I asked Lieutenant Pickering about Dorothy's case (during a call he was expecting), he was not familiar with it. Later, when I asked him why the detective who has had the case since 2012 had—to my knowledge—spoken only with Tonia, Lieutenant Pickering said he could not comment on an ongoing investigation.

A: I've had the case since 2012 and have investigated tips and leads since then, to include recent information that has been developed.

Q: When was the case last reviewed to determine if modern investigative methods—primarily newer technologies or forensic testing—could produce new potential leads?

A: The UHU was formed in 2016. Each primary detective was asked to evaluate their cases in an effort to determine if any new technology could be leveraged to identify new avenues for investigation and to identify what else could be done to push each case forward. The primary detectives are responsible for knowing their unsolved cases and work in conjunction with the UHU to work them.

> The last public record of the case being reviewed was in an article in the *Sun-Journal* on February 11, 1996, quoting Assistant Attorney General Thomas Goodwin: "The 19-year-old murder of Dorothy Milliken in Lewiston received a full review by state and local police this week. Purpose was to bring investigators that have been involved in the case up to speed on what developments have been over the past year, and to plot out some directions that are important to follow up on at this time."
>
> Dr. Margaret Greenwald, the state's former chief medical examiner (ME) from 1998 to 2014, said depending on what evidence is available, unsolved cases are periodically reviewed. The detective(s), ME and staff from the crime lab will get together to review a particular one.
>
> Often during those reviews, someone from the crime lab will report to the group on their evaluation as to whether or not it would be helpful to test or retest for DNA. Sometimes, they may have tested a specific piece of evidence just to see if there is any possibility of identifying foreign DNA. Dr. Greenwald never worked on Dorothy's case and cannot say whether or not testing was done.

Q: Outside of DNA, deathbed confessions, and changed relationships that bring someone forward to identify an offender or previously unknown key witness (for example) how are cold cases solved?

A: Unsolved cases are solved by a great deal of hard work and a little bit of luck. Suspects don't want to volunteer that they killed someone. Some witnesses don't want to volunteer info or get involved because they still fear the suspect(s). Evidence identification, collection, and testing 46 years ago is quite different than it is today. Detectives must be intimate with their cases and actively seek the missing puzzle pieces that complete the picture. Sometimes that comes in the form of retesting evidence with new procedures. Other times, it's working through biases and preconceived ideas to identify other viable suspects. Detectives don't wait around for the deathbed confession—we actively seek new ways to solve cases but sadly, there are often complex reasons why cases go cold, which we have to overcome.

WHEN CHAVEZ SAYS UNSOLVED cases are solved by a great deal of hard work and a little bit of luck, it's unclear what that hard work could be. Reexamining a case by studying the several-inch-thick investigation binders? That seems like an excellent use of time, but if no one from the UHU is reinterviewing people involved in these cases, how are theories vetted? It seems like a missed opportunity to not talk to people. Though some of their memories may have faded, they might also feel more encouraged to talk to law enforcement after so much time has passed. Building relationships with the people involved could develop trust and help with understanding the complexities of situations that were possibly never documented and are thus absent from those police binders. In Dorothy's case, it's not too late to learn who she was, who Peter is and what makes people central to the investigation tick.

THE FORENSICS

A compact grassy campus in Augusta houses the Maine State Police Crime Laboratory, the headquarters for the state police and the offices of the state's chief medical examiner.

The crime lab's main entrance features a realistic nearly floor-to-ceiling painting of a crime scene reconstruction, complete with three crime techs in blue lab coats, a bloody pair of scissors and a body outline. Down a flight of stairs are the labs with state-of-the-art equipment and offices, the latter furnished in the bare-bones style. There is a large snack and meeting room, with an emphasis on snacks. The hall that runs the length of the building is lined with color photographs of forensic teams. There are also two trophy cases filled with early twentieth-century firearms and machine guns, the latter the style pictured in old black-and-white gangster movies.

Maine's crime lab is divided into multiple sections: Forensic Chemistry, Forensic Biology, Firearms/Toolmarks and Latent Prints. The education of the staff ranges from bachelor's degrees in biology, chemistry, forensic science, and clinical laboratory science to master's degrees in various disciplines. They are civilian scientists, not sworn law enforcement officers. They analyze physical evidence, consult databases, read case files, provide updates and insights to detectives and on occasion give expert testimony in court. In the DNA lab, forensic biologists perform the highly sensitive and crucial work of generating a DNA profile from a crime scene stain that might be as tiny as the size of a pinhead. Some teach classes about how to do this stuff.

The unspoken rule here—the primary motivator if you will—is that "every contact leaves a trace." This is Dr. Edmond Locard's exchange principle. The French criminologist, who lived between 1877 and 1966, is considered to be the father of forensic science. His principle holds that whenever the perpetrator of a crime brings something to the crime scene, they'll leave something behind.

Renowned criminologist Paul Kirk (1902–1970), an admirer of Locard's exchange principle, said, "Wherever he steps, whatever he touches, whatever he leaves, even unconsciously, will serve as a silent witness against him."

What did Dorothy's killer leave behind of him or herself?

Alison Gingras

The member of the state's crime lab with the most history is Alison Gingras, a born and bred Mainer, who first came to the lab in the mid-1980s when the offices were in the basement of the state police headquarters next door. She left the lab at one point and returned thirteen years later. Gingras is a forensic chemist who loves being in the lab, on the microscope, and solving puzzles. She says she gets into the work and time just disappears.

Gingras is currently assigned to the UHU. For a case like Dorothy's, she might reanalyze biological matter collected from the scene and determine if anything is worth testing with updated DNA profiling technology.

First, she says she does a visual examination of items to see if there are any stains. What she cannot see with her naked eye in bright light, she then looks at using alternative light sources, including ultraviolet and infrared. If she finds body fluids such as semen, blood or saliva, those can be screened for DNA.

DNA Fingerprinting

In the late 1970s and certainly by the early 1980s, scientists routinely determined species and, if human, the blood group on dried blood samples. Protein electrophoresis—a test used to find abnormal substances—was also done by some laboratories, such as the FBI Laboratory, which Maine's crime lab utilized as necessary.

Deoxyribonucleic acid, or DNA, is a modern key to solving decades-old cold cases.

In September 1984, Sir Alec Jeffreys, a thirty-four-year-old geneticist at the University of Leicester, discovered the technique of genetic fingerprinting. This is the biological identification of any individual using only a minute sample of their DNA. In a landmark case in England in 1986, police asked Jeffreys for help catching the person who murdered two fifteen-year-old girls. DNA tests exonerated a seventeen-year-old with learning disabilities and, through a genetic dragnet, identified the perpetrator.

DNA can be found in everything from dandruff and hair to saliva, sweat and blood.

When DNA profiling first started being used in forensics, the sample size needed was large compared to what technicians can work with today. In the 1980s, when DNA was first used for crime solving, the amount of bloodstain needed by a technician was the size of a dime. With hairs, they needed a clump of pulled hair. Today's DNA analysis methods are much more sensitive, and technicians often work with minute samples. It's also known now that even talking over or breathing over evidence can potentially cause contamination.

Dorothy's DNA

By the mid-'90s, officials were saying publicly that physical evidence would not solve this case. This could have been because of early mishandling of the evidence, the technology did not exist or any number of reasons.

Dorothy bled profusely, so it's possible her blood could have overwhelmed whatever DNA might have been present from the perpetrator.

While questions have been raised regarding how certain items from the scene were stored, the bloodwork was packaged and stored according to best practice standards of the time. Those standards have changed, especially since DNA technology entered the sphere of forensic science. If there were usable DNA samples to test, they have been used up. Other biological evidence (the blood-covered clothing she was wearing) was supposedly stored in plastic. Up until the 1980s or 1990s, whether evidence was collected in paper or plastic depended on who was processing the scene. It is now known that biological evidence should be packaged in paper bags or boxes because paper breathes. If stored in plastic, it will not get air and everything will degrade.

*At some point while in storage, items from another crime scene were mixed in with some of Dorothy's, thus contaminating them. So even if they had been packaged in paper, they would be considered unreliable and inadmissible in court.

Cynthia D. Homer

The coolest person at the crime lab is Cynthia Homer, otherwise known as "Cindy the Red," the latent print supervisor and technical manager and a senior scientist.

The shelves of her office and desktop are covered with action figures of characters from Marvel's Universe and monsters from Universal's classic movies. "They're fun, and that helps," Homer shares.

> *This is an incredibly stressful job, and there are days where I'm just so stressed out that I find it helpful that I can just turn around and look at my action figures. They bring me back to a time when you're a kid and [there was] make believe. It brings me out of this dire world for a little while. Batman is my favorite superhero. I like him because he doesn't have any superpowers. He's just a human that has dedicated himself to helping people.*

Homer is responsible for overseeing the daily operations of the Latent Print section. This includes latent fingerprint examination, trainings and coordinating performance evaluations of supporting staff.

Latent prints, also referred to as crime scene impressions, are formed when the body's natural oils and sweat on the skin are deposited onto a foreign surface. Fingerprint examiners like Homer look for the actual ridge detail that's on a person's finger and then how that ridge detail translates over to an impression it makes. Homer likes to tell people it's like a rubber stamp.

"How we do comparisons is we look for areas where the ridges merge and divide as well as the structure of the ridges." She explains, "Looking at ridges is so much more than them starting and stopping. You're looking at overall shapes of the ridges, how the pores are structured in the ridges."

In addition to fingerprints, Homer and her team also examine other crime scene impressions, like those made by shoes or tires. For all of these they study pattern evidence, which is when an object comes into contact with a surface and that object leaves an impression of itself on that surface. That impression is a representation of that item.

Sometimes police officers don't like what Homer and her team find or don't find. The officer will want the evidence to prove something contrary to what her team has found:

> *I had a guy standing out in the hall, and he's saying, "I have the arrest warrant written up I just need you to tell me that it's this guy's fingerprint," and I'm like, "It's not his fingerprint."…He says, "No, you need to tell me it's his fingerprint because I've already written up the warrant." And I'm like, "It's not his fingerprint." People get really mad at us. I once had a police officer get mad at me for a footwear case. I told him the shoe he had submitted from the suspect did not make the impression at the crime scene. He was the chief of police up in one of the northern police departments and he was so livid at me, and he said, "Well I don't know what kind of fancy equipment you have down there, but I have a photocopier and I can tell that's the same shoe." No, it was not.*

Question Everything

In addition to her full-time position in the lab, Homer also finds time to teach a university-level forensics course. She tells her students to question everything, including the information somebody is giving them, regardless of the credentials that person has or the number of letters they have behind their name. That's not what makes the person, she says—it's how credible are they over time and have they shown that credibility in multiple instances. Homer maintains everybody can tell the truth once. She's been doing this for over two decades and still wants to be questioned. That's how science works she believes, and so she is OK with police questioning her—it's just when they then get an answer they don't like and don't believe the evidence things can get stressful.

CSI Effect

Processing a crime scene and the resulting evidence is not a solve-it-in-an-hour process. Unlike on television shows, it can take a team of people months to do the work that one crime scene tech accomplishes during one episode of the popular CBS show *CSI* and its spin-offs.

Other misconceptions are that the same people who process scenes do the laboratory analysis, interview witnesses and investigate the case. Also, that computers do everything. In real life, Homer says, human beings still have to go through the results.

"People believe what they see on television forgetting it's entertainment," Homer says.

> *Though admittedly there's a lot of reality in it. There are murders and there are forensic scientists, and we do use fingerprints and chemistry and we do examine hairs and fibers. We do all these things, but also, it's a TV show and they have a time limit and have to make it interesting so that people pay attention to it. It's when you end up with people on juries who think that's real and they have those expectations of us—i.e. when a juror asks, "Why didn't you use this whosafradgit machine that I saw on* CSI*?" and we're like, "It doesn't exist," or "How about we can't even afford something that is like that." They might be able to afford it at the FBI, but the State of Maine is not going to buy something like that for a case that might be a one-off case here.*

Homer adds that juries will expect every item of evidence collected from a crime scene to be examined and tested and that if it's not then they believe the police and crime lab have done a shoddy job.

> *At a crime scene you have no idea what has happened. You're trying to identify what might be evidence here. You might miss something and two weeks later find out from an interview the victim carried a red duffle bag. You go back through the crime scene photographs to see was there a red duffel bag there? It's very easy to not pick up a piece of evidence that might be useful down the line because you have no idea. There is no malice involved. It's that they are trying to do their best in figuring out what is important here.*
>
> *I think an important thing I'd want readers to know is that forensic scientists are scientists first. We don't see ourselves as an "arm of the*

law." We don't work for the prosecution or law enforcement, even if the name of the lab suggests otherwise. We use science to interpret the evidence, and we speak for the evidence. We use our science background to solve puzzles and answer questions. We help the justice system by providing answers. Sometimes those answers help the prosecution; sometimes they help the defense. Most of us don't pay much attention to case outcomes; we are more concerned that the evidence is presented and used accurately."

4

THE UNKNOWN

THE THEORIES

In the decades since death came for Dorothy Milliken in that laundromat parking lot in the middle of the night, theories have persisted. They've grown tentacles. Created a labyrinth. There are those theories spoken out loud in public places and those hushed away behind closed doors. Some half-assed from people who never knew Dorothy. It was organized crime. It was the Connecticut River Valley Killer—an unidentified serial killer associated with a number of unsolved murders in the Connecticut River Valley in the 1970s and 1980s. It was a yet-to-be-identified serial killer. It was a lovestruck police officer. It was the jealous husband. It was one of the husband's best friends who went home covered in blood and whose mother admitted as much on her deathbed. It was a transient. The laundromat was where drug deals went down, and Dorothy witnessed something she shouldn't have. Dorothy was about to inform on someone doing back-alley deals with the local cops. At one point early on, a short-lived rumor was that this was the Lewiston Black Dahlia.

In the weeks after Dorothy was killed, people were on edge. Surely detectives working the case would've found someone who heard or saw something. They did, but they are not sharing that information—possibly because it is a delicate situation or because whatever the person(s) saw or heard doesn't connect the dots.

To Dorothy's loved ones, there's nothing reassuring in the hypotheticals. As the years have passed, they've dismissed some angles and held tight to a few.

Consider the who, what, when, where and why of this case. More fact-based, less conjecture.

Who: Dorothy

She could be headstrong and was generally fearless. Her carefree risk-taking days were left behind when she became a mother, but if Dorothy saw something she didn't like or thought was strange, she'd say something whether or not she knew the person(s). Alone in the early hours, Dorothy was not likely to have backed away. If really pissed off—say if someone made a pass at her—she might even have tried kicking them in the groin. This is according to her family and friends. And to be clear, no one is insinuating what happened is remotely Dorothy's fault.

Family who knew she was struggling with a lot at the time—unpaid bills, a sick child, a troubled second marriage—say she went to the laundromat alone that night to clear her mind. Even if the place did have a reputation as a location where people dealt drugs—something that has been suggested by a couple people, but only the police would be able to confirm—she would not have been intimidated out of going there. She was almost desperate for a quiet space to think things through. There is no evidence to support she was having an affair. Also consider that going to the laundromat, or anywhere for that matter, late at night was not usual for her—she was a night owl. She'd stay up cleaning her home until after midnight according to family members. Dorothy, they say, didn't need a lot of sleep.

What

In his book *The Unknown Darkness*, former FBI profiler Gregg O. McCrary writes about victim and offender interactions, how a "triggering event" can turn a normal encounter into a violent homicide. "Overkill," which is thought of as an emotional response—a frenzied act committed in the throes of homicidal rage—could actually be a calculated risk to ensure a witness does not survive. The key for investigators is not to make assumptions and not rule someone out based on any specific item.

There's no telling whether what happened to Dorothy was more emotional response or calculated risk, but clearly both should be considered.

When

At that time of night and in the early morning hours, anyone familiar with the laundromat would have known it would be likely Dorothy would be alone or at the very least that the chance of anyone being there was slim. There was no overnight attendant. If someone wanted to talk to her alone—say away from her husband—then the laundromat would make sense. But to go there to murder her doesn't. As mentioned in the chapter "It's Always the Husband," there are plenty of back roads in Maine with abandoned fields and barns and thick trees where one could do away with someone, places where no one will hear someone scream or see anything, where someone can take their time.

Could someone have driven by and seen her there alone? Maybe, and maybe they went in to talk to her and things went wrong fast.

Or maybe someone who knew the area just needed a bathroom and knew there was one there that was accessible. And they didn't plan for Dorothy, or anyone for that matter, to be there.

Where

Dorothy was killed outside. Back to the stranger theory—what if someone Dorothy didn't know came into the laundromat and she engaged and realized too late this was a dangerous situation and went outside to create space? Maybe she was trying to get to her car. The perpetrator followed her, and things went sideways fast—either because he was out of his mind or didn't want to leave behind a witness. This is an alternate theory to the one that has her husband coming at her in a jealous rage. Or maybe she did know the person and that's why she went out into the night. That seems particularly iffy, because it was really cold and she'd left her jacket inside. Why wouldn't she have taken the time to grab it, even if she was pissed off with whoever showed up and was hurrying outside to them. It would have taken a second to grab—a second that she might not have taken if she was running for her life.

Dorothy's body was left at the site where she was killed. It was moved a few feet and leaned up against the exterior of the building by the unlocked side entrance and not pulled inside further out of view. Keep in mind there were no security cameras outside or inside at that time. If Dorothy's body had been moved inside, it would likely not have been discovered till at least a couple hours later.

McCrary points out that leaving a body outside is risky, which is why killers who do that will typically choose an area with which they're familiar. That seems like common sense, right? Why go to a place you don't know and risk being interrupted or caught? Crime scenes are high-risk environments and none more so than a homicide scene. Offenders typically want to get in and out as quickly as possible for fear of being interrupted or caught.

If one abides by this theory, then the perpetrator might have lived or worked in the area. Maybe they went to the nearby McDonald's or shopped in the supermarket a block down the street. Maybe they even did their laundry there. This would also fit with the timing. Someone who knew the area would be aware of the frequency of traffic on the streets around the laundromat, might know generally when neighborhood newspaper, bread and milk deliveries were. That on a Saturday night in Lewiston, the cops might be preoccupied downtown. Of course, it's also possible they were out of their mind—say on drugs—and weren't thinking clearly.

What does where the murder happened tell us about suspect's mobility? Did they drive, and if so, where would they have parked? On a nearby residential street? In the parking lot of a local business? That would tend toward the homicide being premeditated. Riding a bicycle or walking seems a bit far-fetched unless they lived in the neighborhood or near it. A taxi is even unlikelier, because that could easily be traced. This case was front-page above-the-fold news, and everyone was talking about it—no way would a cab operator miss it.

The weapon was one of convenience, so, while a big question mark, it is not relevant to the *where* of the murder. So as not to compromise the investigation, the weapon will not be identified. It was metal, heavy and something anyone would have access to—but not necessarily something most people would have in their vehicle on any given day. Definitely not something you'd walk down the street with.

Whoever attacked Dorothy used their fists and a metal object. If their goal wasn't to kill her, would they have relied on their fists?

Why

This is the murkiest of all the questions. There is so much about crime fighting that wasn't known in 1976. But the basics about why people murdered people were known— love, treasure/greed or revenge. Those haven't changed. Dorothy wasn't robbed, so that could rule out treasure.

Organized Crime, Drugs and the Informant Angle

In 1979, Detective Rafnell said the rumor that organized crime was involved in Dorothy's murder could not be substantiated. Conversations for this book also gave no indication whatsoever that Dorothy was ever directly involved in any illegal activities.

In the summer of 1976, local cars were being stolen, and rumor has it that there was an organized crime contact paying off Lewiston police officers. The police involved secured legitimate vehicle identification numbers to attach to the stolen cars to make them seem like they were legit cars that could then be sold. No interviewees gave the impression that there were significant changes in any of Dorothy's relationships with persons who might have been involved. Nothing to indicate she was pissed off with anyone enough to go to the police about them—something she hadn't done even when she was angry with somebody known to regularly be involved in nefarious deals.

When Dorothy returned to the Sabattus area in 1968, a childhood classmate said she confided in him that she was nervous about something and he speculated it was over drugs. He got the impression that someone around her—likely Gerald—was possibly involved in drug trafficking, but not her. More than anything, it seemed to him like she was struggling with whether to say something or maybe distance herself from him. That one interaction is the only one he had to base these thoughts on, and it took place years before Dorothy was murdered, when she was in a relationship with Gerald.

A former member of law enforcement said whenever someone who worked in the medical field was killed, that part of the investigation always involved looking into what access they had to drugs and if there were any discrepancies. This was more routine than anything. As a dental assistant,

Dorothy would have some access, but if she was doing anything illegal, there's not a whiff of it.

Former law enforcement not involved in Dorothy's case said the laundromat could have been an attractive place to deal drugs because there was no attendant at night and people would pass through. Any place that's got people coming and going, they said, would potentially be a good outlay for drugs. Some interviews did suggest word on the street might have been the laundromat was at least nocturnally and on limited occasions a place where drugs were dealt. This theory is far from concrete, and it's relevant to note Dorothy had been in the laundromat for a couple hours when she was killed, so it's not like she walked in on anything or surprised anyone.

One need only look at Dorothy's willingness to marry Gerald, who had killed an innocent person, and then married Peter, who was known to hang out with criminals, to surmise her being an informant was highly unlikely.

The Police Officer

Police have never publicly stated this individual was a person of interest in any murder. Newspaper articles around the time of Dorothy's death do not mention his name; however, it does come up in later coverage. He was not approached for this book.

Kenneth Richard Gilman was born in 1950. While he was a member of the ski team at Hall-Dale High School in Farmington, he would have had access to some of the best skiing in Maine. He didn't just ski though; he played football, was in the band and the chorus, was on the track team, was a member of the Glee Club and the Key Club, participated in the yearbook committee and on the Winter Carnival three years in a row. He was even a member of the Hokey Pokey Stage Crew his senior year. He was thin, of average height, and wore glasses; vacant eyes stare out in yearbook photos, where he looks slightly uncomfortable.

Following his active stint in high school, which concluded in 1968, he worked for Central Maine Power and attended the Maine Maritime Academy. Then in September 1972, he found his calling and joined the town of Hallowell's police department, which he left a few months later for the larger police force in Lewiston. And then tragedy struck. On September 15, 1973, his eighteen-year-old girlfriend, Debra, left her job at an Augusta department store and was scheduled to begin another part-time job at a pizza joint. She never showed. Hours later, Debra was found bludgeoned and possibly strangled to death within twenty feet of her blue Ford Falcon on a wooded backcountry road near the Monmouth-Litchfield line. Many homes in the area were summer residences, and only a few were occupied after Labor Day. Ninety minutes before her estimated time of death, Gilman had been with Debra. She'd shown him wedding invitations, although it's not clear if the couple was actually engaged. Gilman was interviewed, passed at least one polygraph and was alibied out by a fellow officer. In 1991, another man by the name of Michael Boucher was tried and convicted for Debra's murder in Kennebec County Superior Court. He died in prison in 2022.

Lyndon Abbott, who interviewed Gilman in 1973, says he was a braggart and told officers in a Dunkin' Donuts in Lewiston about a woman he was dating at one time: "See that girl out there in the car, if any of you want a piece of tail, boy she's a good one."

Abbott spoke with eighteen to twenty Lewiston cops about Gilman in 1973 and asked each who disliked him the most. He found that officer and confirmed Gilman had been at an authentic stop. "Yes, Gilman called me because he's gutless and to back him up and he didn't really need it," the officer said. The stop was out of Lewiston on Route 126 but not as far as Whippoorwill Road in Litchfield near where Debra's body was found.

Fast-forward to November 5, 1976. Gilman was still a Lewiston cop. In fact, he was assigned to the morning shift that secured Dorothy's crime scene. Only, he was not on duty. Instead, he was fixing his car a block down and across the street from the laundromat at Healy's Garage, which was leased by a friend of his, a family guy who lived in the town over and would occasionally let friends work on their cars at the garage after hours. From this gas station, one has a clear view of the location where Dorothy was killed. According to Mark LaFlamme's article in the February 19, 2001 edition of the *Sun Journal*, police reports have Gilman saying he was spray painting and applying putty to his car the morning of the murder. He said he heard a loud noise in the area of the laundromat at around 2:00 a.m. and described a dark-colored car that slowed and turned around near Dumont Avenue around the same time. According to the report, as described in the article, he didn't pay attention to it and continued working on his car until around 4:00 a.m., at which point he went home. William Welch, who was a Lewiston police officer in 1976, acknowledged that Gilman was questioned in the case as a possible witness.

DEBRA AND DOROTHY LOOKED remarkably alike—so much so they could have been sisters. However, there is no evidence of Gilman and Dorothy ever meeting. Unless they met that fateful night: Dorothy could have gone across the street to Healy's Garage while Gilman was there working on his car to get a can of Pepsi from the soda vending machine. There wasn't a soda machine at the laundromat, but there was at the gas station. A can of Pepsi was found with Dorothy's things in the laundromat.

ANOTHER VERSION OF THE STORY

Most investigations are not like Agatha Christie stories. From the beginning, this case kept feeling like what happened to Dorothy was more straightforward than it was being made out to be. Why would someone who had been around her for years and could have chosen any time to kill her not done so before? Why that night? Why in such a visible space? Consider the laundromat was surrounded by homes and situated on a busy street. And then there's the sheer brutality of how she was killed.

One person involved in the case said, "She was there doing her clothes, and somebody didn't like her. She just happened to be in the place she shouldn't be in." Maybe, or maybe Dorothy was just in the wrong place at the wrong time, and it had nothing to do with a personal vendetta—nothing to even do with her.

What it boils down to is this: Was the murderer a serial offender who has not been discovered or who no one knows was in town that weekend or a psychopath who killed once, maybe twice, that weekend and never again? Both sound fantastic. Which is easier to believe?

Did investigators have everything they needed to solve Dorothy's murder back in 1976?

What if the person who killed her was not some deceitful mastermind or dysfunctional killer but an unstable, cold-blooded twenty-year-old man who had been out with friends for a wild night of drinking and doing drugs, gotten blood on himself while killing an old man for seventy dollars, gone to a twenty-four-hour laundromat to wash up and run into a young mother of three doing her laundry, a young woman who would have questioned what she saw and not backed down if challenged. What if the state police dismissed the connection immediately because she wasn't robbed, because all law enforcement agencies engaged were overwhelmed and the authorities were focused on the husband pretty much from the get-go?

Isn't it the least bit strange that the exact same type of murder happened in the same town on the same night in a place that very rarely ever saw these types of murders? How could it be a coincidence?

According to news reports, that's exactly what law enforcement seemed to think it was, because at noon that Saturday—only a few hours after both bodies were discovered—DA Thomas Delahanty told the press that, as of yet, there was no reason to assume any connection between the death of McBride and the early morning death of Dorothy Milliken.

By Monday, the police were declining to comment on the evidence that led them to arrest twenty-year-old Scott B. Snow. He was apprehended on Sunday night at Deborah Farrington's apartment at 56½ Shawmut Street in Lewiston for the murder of Robert McBride, sixty-nine, of Springvale at the Lewiston Fairgrounds on Saturday. The authorities continued to say there was no apparent relationship between McBride's murder and Dorothy's.

In early December, Deputy Attorney General Richard Cohen said authorities were proceeding with interviewing people as part of the investigation into Dorothy's murder. He also said for the first and possibly only time that state and local investigators had not dismissed the possibility that the two murders might be related. He admitted it seemed more than just a coincidence and said it was being looked into hard. Of course, he also indicated that the police had not identified the weapon used in Dorothy's murder, when, in fact, it was very likely they had. Interestingly, Cohen also acknowledged that law enforcement was dealing with more stranger versus "lover-related" types of murders. This would have certainly taxed investigators.

In early February 1977, two months before Snow's homicide trial, Cohen maintained the state had nothing concrete to show that the two cases were connected.

Takes the Fifth

During the probable cause hearing of Snow on November 22, 1976, in the small Eighth District Court, Daniel Farrington, who had been with Snow the night of the McBride murder, refused to answer the state's questions on the grounds his answers might incriminate him. Lewiston attorney Coleman Coyne, who represented Farrington, advised his client to plead the fifth based on his not being familiar with the details of the case.

State v. Snow

The following is taken from April 5, 1978 (Maine case law) 383 A.2d 1385—*STATE of Maine v. Scott B. SNOW*—Maine Supreme Court:

> *On the afternoon of November 5, 1976, the Defendant first met Robert "Shorty" McBride at a Lewiston second-hand store. The Defendant was trying to sell some stereo speakers when McBride approached in an intoxicated state and requested a ride so he could cash a check. Although the "request" was originally addressed to the store owner, the Defendant eventually agreed to drive McBride in exchange for $5.00.*
>
> *The two drove to the Lewiston fairgrounds, where McBride lived in the tackroom of one of the barns, to pick up the check, and from there they proceeded to a store in Greene where McBride cashed a Social Security check in the amount of $106.00. The Defendant drove McBride back to Lewiston and dropped him off in the downtown area.*

Ultimately, Daniel Farrington was granted immunity from prosecution. Following is a summary of the description he gave the jury in the Androscoggin Superior Court during Snow's homicide trial in late March and early April 1977 regarding the events of November 5 and 6:

FARRINGTON GOT OFF WORK in Monmouth around 3:00 p.m. and went to the home of Blaine Richards (also in Monmouth). They started drinking, and then went to Winthrop and back to Monmouth, where Arnold Libby of Winthrop joined the group. Later, around 9:30 p.m., Farrington said he went to his sister Deborah's home in Lewiston, where he met up with Snow. Farrington, Snow and Libby then drank some more and smoked pot.

Farrington bought two speakers from Snow for twenty-five dollars and then drove Libby's car to Lisbon, where they purchased three six-packs of beer. Later, Farrington, Snow and Libby went into a field or gravel pit, where they continued smoking pot and drinking beer. Then they went to the Disco. There he and Snow bought more beer.

From the Disco, Farrington took Libby, who had passed out, home to Monmouth by way of Route 202. Later, under cross-examination by attorney William H. Clifford Jr., Farrington admitted he had been driving at speeds around 120 miles per hour and had passed a state trooper on the side of the road.

From Libby's home, Snow and Farrington got into the latter's Volkswagen and drove to the Lewiston fairgrounds, where they arrived around two o'clock in the morning. Snow then told Farrington he was going "into the barn to take some guy's money." Farrington said Snow asked him if he had a tire iron because "there was some drunk old man in there and he wanted to hit him and take his money." After Farrington told him he didn't have a tire iron, Snow was seen leaning over like he was looking for something and went back in the barn. When he came back out two or three minutes later, he told Farrington he'd hit the guy and reached into his pocket to get the cash.

Farrington said Snow lit a match and saw some blood and told him he thought he killed the man. At this time, Snow gave Farrington ten dollars, and then they went to Farrington's sister's and spent the night there.

In the morning, Snow got up first and went to a store for a couple of Italian sandwiches. Later in the day, they purchased a water pump for Snow's car, which he installed at his mother's house.

During the day, they heard on the radio that McBride was dead. Farrington said he tried to talk to Snow about what happened, but he didn't want to talk about it.

Notes re: Farrington's Testimony

Farrington's reference to "the Disco" is Disco 2000, which was located at 2151 Lisbon Street on the outskirts of Lewiston. The place served beer and pizza till midnight. Drinks had to be off the table by 1:00 a.m. It was packed on weekends, attracting coeds from Bates College and young sailors from the Brunswick Naval Air Station. Underage partiers (between

1972 and 1977, the drinking age was eighteen) who couldn't get in hung out outside in the big dirt parking lot. The Disco opened in 1972 and closed in 1977.

One of the former owners of Disco 2000 doesn't recall any officer ever asking him or any of his partners about a homicide. Is it possible the police did not follow up on Snow's supposed movements leading up to the murder?

Chances are they'd have driven through Lewiston past the laundromat and seen it lit up on their way from Disco 2000 to Route 202. From the nightclub, taking main streets to Route 202, they'd have left 2151 Lisbon Road traveling along Lisbon Street/Route 196 and passed the laundromat on their left before taking a right onto East Avenue, which they could have taken up several blocks before turning left onto Montello Street, which would have taken them right by the fairground (good opportunity to survey the scene) before hopping onto Route 202.

There is no follow-up in any media coverage regarding the state trooper. It is possible there is an explanation and/or name in the court transcript. It seems strange Farrington would have lied about the state trooper.

Dr. Ryan's autopsy report estimated McBride had been dead about six hours when examined shortly after 9:00 a.m. Dorothy was believed to have been killed in the early hours; however, no exact time was ever released.

Dr. Ryan testified it was impossible to tell how many blows McBride had received, and postmortem tests showed the alcohol content of his blood to be .12 percent. With a blood alcohol level of .10 percent or higher, a person is at risk of blacking out. Not only did Snow beat an old man to death, but the man might also have been passed out when he did it.

If when Farrington was under cross-examination he was asked what happened between the time he and Snow left the fairgrounds and arrived at the apartment in Lewiston, that was not in the press coverage.

Consider if Snow went to the laundromat to wash the blood off his hands. Maybe he'd seen the lights on at the laundromat and knew it was open and likely had a bathroom and went there. He probably wasn't going in with violent intent and certainly not to do robbery. But what if Dorothy saw him—a messed-up guy with blood on him—and said something? What if he panicked? What if they engaged and things went sideways?

Violent Man May Not Remember

At some point on Saturday, authorities questioned Farrington about McBride's murder. Later that evening, police called the longtime owner of the apartment building at 56 Shawmut Street in Lewiston and asked him to evacuate the tenants because they suspected whoever murdered McBride was hiding in one of the apartments. He was elderly and quite shaken by that call and subsequent events, his daughter shares. She collected rents and says back then they got a lot of "riffraff" renting one-bedroom apartments. Aside from that event, however, she never felt unsafe in the area.

By Sunday evening, Farrington had decided to go with his parents to the Lewiston police station and then with the police to the fairgrounds to show them where he'd parked his car. Sometime later that evening, Detective Bruce Rafnell arrested Snow with the support of the local cops.

Rafnell also attended Snow's interrogation at Lewiston police headquarters. In court, Rafnell testified that after leaving Farrington's sister's apartment that night, Snow said he didn't know where he went. Years later, a relative of Snow's told a member of Dorothy's family that Snow had taken hard drugs that night and that between those and the alcohol said he couldn't remember murdering anyone. That he had blacked out.

Sentenced

After a four-day trial that opened on March 29, Snow was found guilty of first-degree homicide by a jury of seven men and five women and sentenced by Justice Harold Rubin to life imprisonment at Maine State Prison (formerly in Thomaston).

Snow was paroled in 1985 after serving a little over eight years, at the age of twenty-nine.

UNANSWERED QUESTIONS

Was the information Dorothy Couture gave the police regarding what she saw the morning of Dorothy's murder followed up on?

Have either Daniel Farrington or Scott Snow been questioned regarding Dorothy Milliken's murder? If so, what did they say? If not, why?

What was Daniel Farrington's account to police in 1976 for the hours between 2:00 and 4:00 a.m. on November 6?

Aside from the burglary angle, why was Snow so quickly dismissed as a suspect in Dorothy's murder and Farrington as an accomplice?

Do the state police still have viable evidence from the McBride crime scene, including Snow and Farrington's clothing? Was Farrington's car treated as a crime scene, and if so, is that evidence still viable and available to investigators?

What questions did investigators ask Gail Ann Hinkley? What did she tell them?

Above: Lewiston Police Department's Dispatch Department. *Courtesy of Dave Gudas.*

Left: Lewiston Police Department's Criminal Investigation Office as it looked in 1985 when on the first floor of city hall. Detectives on Dorothy's case would have worked out of this room. *Courtesy of Dave Gudas.*

Opposite, top: *Lewiston Evening Journal* headlines, Saturday, November 6, 1976. *Courtesy of the Sun Journal; photo by Simokaitis.*

Opposite, bottom: Scene of Robert McBride's murder at the Lewiston Fairgrounds. *Courtesy of the Sun Journal; photo by Simokaitis.*

Proverbs Were Bright Shafts In The Greek And Latin Quivers — Disraeli

LEWISTON EVENING JOURNAL

VOLUME 116   Lewiston Weekly Journal Established 1847   Lewiston Evening Journal Established 1861   28 PAGES   LEWISTON-AUBURN, MAINE   SATURDAY, NOVEMBER 6, 1976   LAST EDITION   15 CENTS

Sabattus Mother Is Found Slain In Lewiston

Police Probe Slaying At The Fairgrounds

Body Is Found In Horse Barn

By NANCY GRAPE

A 69-year-old horse handler, who followed the sulky racing circuit around northern New England, was found dead in his bunk in a horse barn at the Lewiston Fairgrounds this morning.

He was Robert B. "Shorty" McBride, and the cause of death, according to District Attorney Thomas E. Delahanty II, was a blow to the head.

It was the second homicide to confront Lewiston Police, Sheriff's detectives and State Police investigators in the city within four hours.

D.A. Delahanty, however, stated at Noon there is, as yet, no reason to assume any connection between the death of McBride and the earlier morning death of Dorothy Milliken near a Lewiston laundromat.

"There doesn't seem to be any apparent connection at that time," Delahanty declared.

Speaking for the combined law enforcement effort which will be working throughout the weekend, Delahanty stated the McBride death was reported at about 8:45 a.m.

The small, grey-haired stablehand, who had been familiar at the Lewiston track for decades working at mucking out stalls and hitching up the race horses, was found wearing his day clothes, lying in his bunk in a cluttered, single-cot room.

A three-foot long, splained two-by-four piece of wood found on the floor nearby was identified by police as the probable weapon used to strike the lethal blow.

According to Delahanty, the condition of McBride's room in the green-trimmed yellow stable, its second floor filled with hay, was such as to make it difficult to determine whether a struggle had taken place there.

The time of death had not yet been determined as officials awaited results of an autopsy to be conducted by Maine Chief Medical Examiner, Dr. Henry F. Ryan at Augusta General Hospital.

"We won't know any more details on that until they do an autopsy this afternoon," Delahanty declared. Hopefully the autopsy may give us the time of death."

At noon today, police had no suspects in the killing, but were questioning persons at the track.

As of a.m., uniformed police and city detectives, led by Chief Lucien Langelier, together with D.A. Delahanty, Sheriff's and state police investigators con-

LEWISTON HOMICIDE SCENE — Mrs. Dorothy Rousseau Milliken was found dead today outside Beal's Laundromat, her body badly beaten. The Sabattus woman's petite body was found shortly before 5 a.m. partially-propped up against the Dumont Avenue side of the all-night cleaning establishment, to the left of the doorway in the picture.

Staff Photo by Simoneau

Authorities shown prepare to tow away the woman's car secured within the roped off area. Authorities said they have no suspect or suspects in the beating death.

ROBERT McBRIDE

Body Discovered At Laundromat

AG, DA's Offices And LPD Conducting Probe

By JAN OBLINGER

The brutally-beaten body of a young Sabattus woman was found early today outside Beal's Laundromat at Lisbon Street and Dumont Avenue in Lewiston.

Authorities identified the victim as Dorothy L. Milliken, 37, of the Pleasant Ridge Road. Her bloodied body was found shortly before 5 o'clock by a man walking his dog, officials said.

District Attorney Thomas E. Delahanty II said it appeared the woman had been badly beaten about the head with an undetermined weapon. The spokesman said there is no suspect as yet.

Asked about motive, the official said there has not been determined. "It could have been anything," he said.

Delahanty, who acted as spokesman for the team of investigators probing the beating death, said the woman left her Sabattus home alone around 3 o'clock to go do her laundry. Her laundry and her car were at the Lisbon Street all-night cleaning establishment, authorities reported.

It was reported that Mrs. Milliken had been in the habit of doing her laundry in the early morning hours.

The woman's body was found clad in a white T-shirt and blue dungarees leaning up against the outside wall of the building on the Dumont Avenue side. She was barefoot. A pair of sandals, believed to be hers, were next to the body, investigators said.

Delahanty said the body was coatless but that a sweater he said belonging to her was found inside the laundry along with a very large bundle of dirty clothes.

The spokesman said the beating apparently took place sometime after 3:30 which is the estimated time of Mrs. Milliken's arrival at the cleaning establishment.

Investigators were attempting to pinpoint the time of the death through questioning of residents at the apartment buildings in the residential area around and behind the Beal Lisbon St. cleaners.

Initial contact with neighbors, Delahanty said, failed to turn up anything which could help police.

Continued On Page 6, Col. 1

Continued On Page 6, Col. 1

DOROTHY MILLIKEN

HAS THE USE OF AN AIR FORCE JET

Carter Is Off On A Vacation

BY LAWRENCE L. KNUTSON
Associated Press Writer

ST. SIMON'S ISLAND, Ga. (AP) — Jimmy Carter got his first official taste of presidential luxury today. Flying in a large blue and silver Air Force plane to a vacation retreat amid the pines and palms of this coastal island.

"This is the one I've been waiting for," said the Carter when he saw the aircraft, emblazoned with the seal of the President of the United States.

"I felt like going back and getting my dayto-piece black

President Richard M. Nixon to China.

As fishing rods and other vacation paraphernalia were loaded, Carter told reporters he will meet with Ford, and his wife, Rosalynn, will meet with Mrs. Ford, before the end of the month.

But before that, he said, he will receive a national security briefing from Central Intelligence Director George Bush.

Among the luggage was a large box marked "transition monuments," and Carter said

pristion for paying expenses involved in transferring leadership from Republican Gerald Ford to Carter.

While at Musgrove Plantation on St. Simon's Island, Carter plans to dig into a huge stack of documents dealing with the appointments and organization of the Carter administration and the policy options that will be available to him as the nation's 39th president.

But Carter plans to use most of his time on the island, which is separated from the Georgia mainland by the Intracoastal

Mrs. Rosalynn Carter and the couple's three sons and their wives will accompany the President-elect.

The estate is owned by Smith Bagley, a grandson of tobacco magnate R. J. Reynolds. A Carter aide said the President-elect will pay Bagley between $1,000 and $2,000 for the use of the estate.

After the daily limelight of the campaign, Carter plans to stay out of the public eye for most of his vacation. Reporters accompanying the President-elect have been advised to us

torn, visited his present warehouse at a nearby farm and worked out details for beefed service protection of his 9-year-old daughter, Amy.

He also was pronounced in good health by his physician after a physical examination.

Carter's press secretary, Jody Powell, said there is a possibility key members of the campaign staff will meet with

One block from the laundromat, which can be seen in the background of the photo where a car is parked. Dorothy's car would have been parked in the same place on November 6, 1976. Photo was taken by unknown photographer in 1970. Spudnuts closed before 1976. *Courtesy of Dave Gudas*.

Downtown Lewiston street in 1985 near city hall. *Courtesy of Dave Gudas*.

Top: The stone marking the graves of Dorothy and her parents. *Image by author.*

Bottom: Retired state police detective Lyndon Abbott in 1986. *Courtesy of the Sun Journal; photo by Cheryl Denz.*

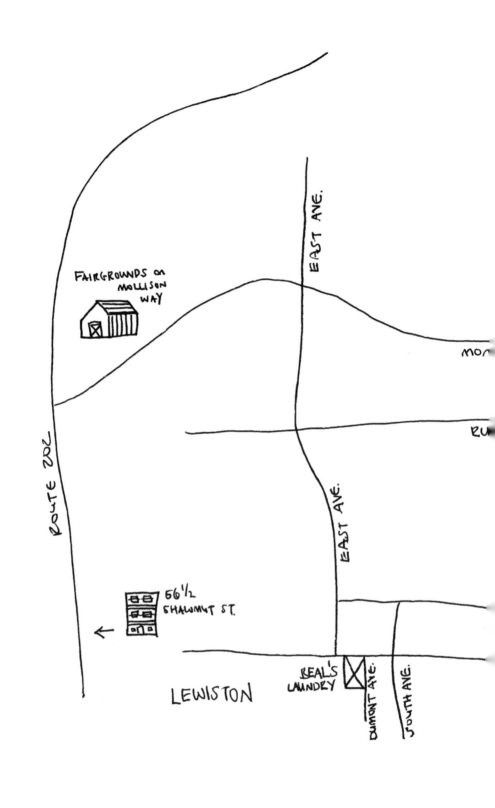

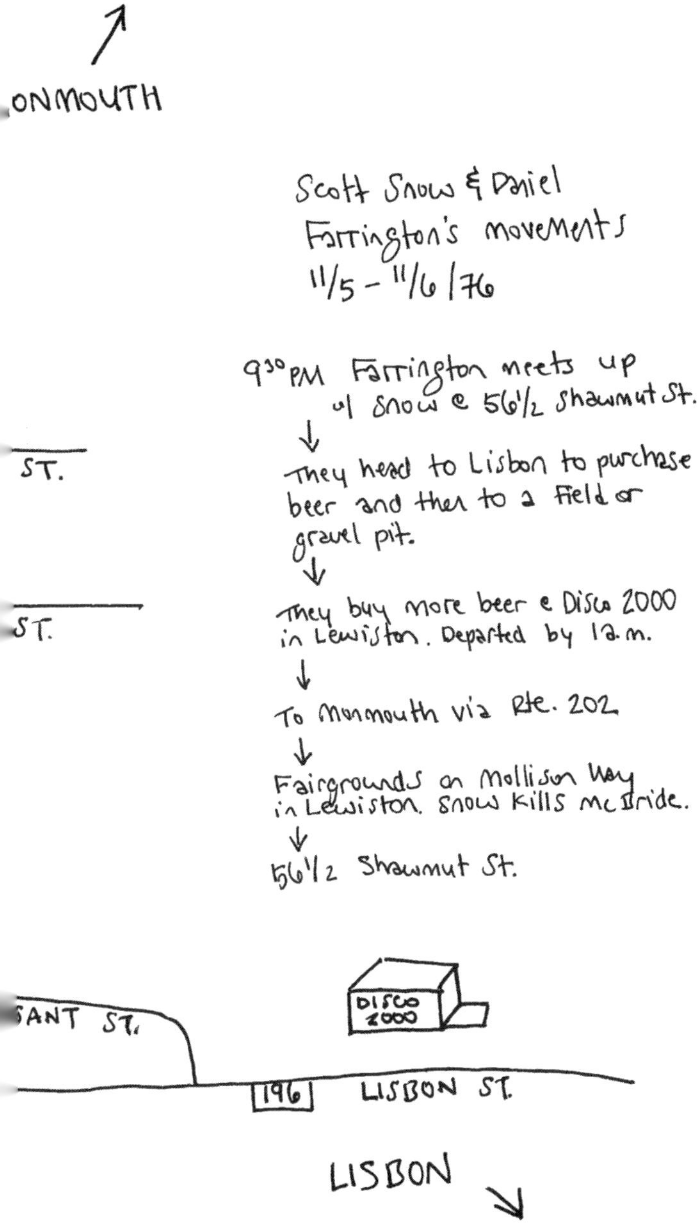

ONMOUTH

Scott Snow & Daniel
Farrington's movements
11/5 - 11/6/76

9³⁰ PM Farrington meets up
        w/ Snow @ 56½ Shawmut St.
        ↓
They head to Lisbon to purchase
beer and then to a field or
gravel pit.
        ↓
They buy more beer @ Disco 2000
in Lewiston. Departed by 12 m.
        ↓
To Monmouth via Rte. 202
        ↓
Fairgrounds on Mollison Way
in Lewiston. Snow kills McBride.
        ↓
56½ Shawmut St.

ST.

ST.

SANT ST.

DISCO 2000

[196] LISBON ST.

LISBON ↓

Hand-drawn
map of the route
Scott Snow and
Daniel Farrington
could have taken
November 5–6,
1976. Much of this is
based on Farrington's
testimony during
Snow's trial in 1977.
Map by author.

Right: Scrapbooks and photo albums at Dorothy's sister Peggy's home. *Image by author*.

Left: Tonia, Erica and baby Pete in 1977 posing for a family portrait. *Courtesy of the Rancourt family*.

Clockwise from top left: Military photos of Dorothy's granddaughter Kayla-Rae, Tonia's daughter, and Dorothy herself, both age eighteen. *Courtesy of Tonia Ross.*

Tonia holding a letter from convicted murderer Michael Boucher. *Courtesy of Tonia Ross.*

Tonia Ross, Dorothy's eldest daughter. *Courtesy of Tonia Ross.*

5

THE SURVIVORS

A life too short. Dorothy was a match blown out before it had a chance to really burn. Every November is a reminder of her heartbreaking absence and the dearth of answers about what really happened that weekend nearly a half-century ago.

The killer, like others of his ilk who have committed murders that remain unsolved, walks free, able to attend family birthday parties, go to baseball games with friends and the rest. Do they feel safe, what they did forgotten by the public? Are they at all guilty? Did they get away with it again? Are they in the ground? Meanwhile, the families of lost loved ones wait—their hope three-hole punched into a large blue binder on the shelf of a state office somewhere.

THE DAUGHTERS

Dorothy's younger daughter, Erica, who was two when her mother died, has no memory of her mother aside from the smell of her. The scent of her laundry soap. She knows what she looked like from photographs and who she was based on stories her aunt Mary Ellen and father, Peter, have passed on to her.

Tonia, the oldest child, has often been told how much she is like her mom. Dorothy's toughness, protectiveness and sense of fun run through her veins. "Growing up, a lot of people told me I was just like my mother," she shares.

After their mother's death, Dorothy's children were divided up between her sisters Mary Ellen and Peggy. Erica and her older sister, Tonia, who was seven at the time, went to live with Peggy; her husband, Moe; and their daughter Heidi in Lewiston. Little Pete went to live with Mary Ellen; her husband, Glen; and daughter Julie and son Glen Jr. in West Bowdoin.

Tonia, who carries a handful of precious memories of her mother, has been shaped by the divide of Dorothy's death—the before and after. When she calls up images of time with her mom, she remembers her smile and laugh, going with her to pick black-eyed Susans and daisies in the front yard, dancing in the kitchen together, her long beautiful nails, her mom painting her nails. "She was a fun person," Tonia recalls. "She was true blue. I can remember her giving me a bar of soap and letting me wash up and play in the rain—letting me be a kid."

Tonia describes her memories of her mom like they are a movie reel in her head. The memories are part of a vortex where pain cohabitates with anger and resentment.

IN HER OWN WORDS, here is an account of a life without her mom:

> *Seven years I had her. She was my mom and someone took her away from me. They had no right, but they did. She was everything that a child could ever ask for in a mother. She loved me, my sister, and brother more than anything in the world. It always felt like there was something missing growing up. The day she was taken everything changed. I always thought she was going to come back. Days passed. Weeks passed. Years passed. She never came. I was fifteen, sixteen, she was never coming back. I was a confused kid. I did things I probably shouldn't have done.*
>
> *She never got to meet my husband or her granddaughters. All things that would have given her so much joy. She didn't choose to leave, she was taken.*
>
> *I still have moments when I cry because I miss my mom so much.*

Tonia has lost her grandparents and brother, Pete. One of Tonia's biggest regrets is that she was not allowed to be Pete's big sister. She'd have loved to have taught him how to fish and tossed the ball with him. Tonia remembers when he was born giving him kisses, holding him and feeding him.

And at the end of his life, when he was lying in the hospital bed, she sang "Amazing Grace" to him and told him to let go and that he needed to "grab momma's hand." That their mother was waiting there for him.

Investigation

During her teenage years, all the anger Tonia was feeling at having her mother taken away from her and living apart from her brother bubbled up. When it reached a boiling-over point, she realized she had to figure out how to get rid of it.

Around her eighteenth birthday in 1987, she began asking questions about what had happened to her mother. She talked with her aunt Mary Ellen and asked her who she thought had killed Dorothy. There was nothing firm to grasp onto at the time, and Tonia kept reaching out to people who knew her mother and asked them about her and if they knew anything. She was relentless in her attempts and talked to dozens of people. But she wasn't getting satisfactory answers.

In 1994, when she was twenty-five, Tonia contacted the Attorney General's Office, which put her in touch with Timothy Culbert, the state detective who had her mother's case at the time. He agreed to let her see the investigative file. This was a rare exception and one no longer available according to Tonia, who has since been denied by the state police another viewing. She asked her stepsister to go with her for emotional support, knowing she cared deeply for Dorothy. They visited the AG's Office in Augusta twice and read as much as they could of the case's antiquated documents. What interested Tonia most were the names of suspects and who had been interviewed and polygraphed.

Within a month or so, Tonia went back with her aunts Mary Ellen and Peggy and uncle Bob and viewed the binders again. During this and her earlier trips, she explains that she had to detach emotionally looking at the information as if it was for an anonymous murder victim. After each visit, she would go home and cry that it was her mom and largely attributes her mother-in-law's loving hand with helping her process her grief and understand what she was feeling.

Ultimately, and Tonia is quick to clarify this is not a criticism of the state police, she didn't feel what she'd read in the files made sense based on what she knew about her mom and had been told by relatives about her mom's murder. With a knack for remembering details like names and years, she had memorized parts of the file and decided—along with her stepsister—to go out and start talking to people whose names she had spotted, dozens of friends and associates her mom had known.

In hindsight, Tonia says she feels this was a bit arrogant, explaining that she didn't really have an organized plan and was hoping to draw the person out, not knowing what she would do then.

Unsolved Mysteries and a Reward

In 1996, Tonia tried to bring exposure to her mother's case by attempting to get it featured on a segment of the NBC show *Unsolved Mysteries*. Tonia and her stepsister collected more than five thousand signatures for a petition to help support her request to have the case featured on the television program. Ultimately, however, producers passed. It was not a total loss though, Tonia's efforts spurred authorities to do a full review of the case—possibly for the first time in nearly two decades.

Eventually, she began writing to inmates, including Michael Boucher, who was sentenced to life imprisonment in 1991 for beating and strangling to death an eighteen-year-old in September 1973.

In November 2006, Tonia and her husband offered a $5,000 reward for information leading to the arrest and conviction of Dorothy's killer. They increased the amount to $10,000, which is where it stands as of January 2025.

In 2014, her grandmother Lois died. A year later, Tonia began learning about Reiki, yoga and shamanism. She credits her husband, whom she married in 1997, becoming a mother to two young women with whom she has a close bond, and her daily practices to her healing.

In 2021, Tonia gave her last interview. On the Portland, Maine–based television station affiliated with NBC, she told the interviewer on the program *News Center Maine* that she believed her mother saw someone she knew well and went outside the laundromat to talk to them. She begged the person to come forward.

At various points over the years—both while doing her own investigating and after—she has been at least 50 percent sure she knew who the murderer was. "In my mind, I can sit there and take all of the suspects, and I go back to one every single time," she says.

In the midst of her research, she became interested in the cases of other women who had been killed—especially those under similar circumstances. When she began to feel the investigation had become an obsession, she boxed up her files, put them in a closet and closed the door. But she didn't lock it.

NOTE: TONIA AND I committed to her not revealing anything she saw in the state's investigative files and my not asking her to. This was our way of respecting the state's decision to not share any information about the case with me. In the end, we feel this worked out for the best, because it possibly made me dig deeper and farther than I might have if biased by what was or was not in those binders.

Where Are They Now?

After 2015, when her brother, Pete, passed away, Erica moved out of state.

Tonia got married in 1997. The couple have two daughters. Tonia and her husband live in Maine. Her passion for painting and photography has turned into a hobby.

THE BABY

Peter Arron Milliken, nicknamed "little Pete," was born on Sunday, August 15, 1976. His aunt Mary Ellen and her husband, Glen, became his "beloved parents" who raised him after Dorothy died. Mary Ellen describes him as having been a happy baby. She says, however, that when he returned from Presque Isle, where he'd been with Peter and his girlfriend for the better part of a year, he was suddenly unnaturally afraid of water. Peggy inserts that when Erica, then a toddler, returned, she was terrified of the moon. They believe Peter told the children stories to make them afraid.

As little Pete grew, he enjoyed fishing and sports. As he grew older, he began to get in trouble with the law for variety of misdemeanors, including theft. From time to time, he would do things to get incarcerated intentionally to find his mother's killer. Tonia says her brother was perhaps hoping to find a jailhouse snitch who had heard something.

He died of natural causes at age thirty-eight the morning of February 14, 2015, in Bangor, Maine.

THE SIBLINGS

Mary Ellen and Peggy were Dorothy's closest friends, and the loss those two women feel has been palpable. Mary Ellen lives in their childhood home and sees her sister in the fields and trees. Peggy has been entrusted with Erica's photo albums and the scrapbooks she inherited from Dorothy. All are well-worn and dust-free.

They are fiercely protective of their sister and are always able to offer up special insights.

"After she was killed, I got notices of layaways for clothes for her girls and the baby and even Peter," Peggy shares. "She made sure they were going to have stuff that was warm at Christmas. Little sleepers and things. She wanted her family to be warm." Peggy says that was Dorothy, always organized and trying to take care of her family.

George, who is seven years younger than Dorothy, remembers his sister as his protector, stepping between him and anyone who might try to rough him up. Always there to boost his confidence. "She would tell me, you know if the president of the United States was here, he'd be no better than you," George says.

His memories are clear as day, like the time he was in a field by the farm with Dorothy and Mary Ellen. "They said go make us some peanut butter sandwiches and we'll wait for you," he shares. "And when I got back, they were gone. I think they were going to go smoke cigarettes and didn't want me around."

For Bob, it was an especially hard loss, because just a few months before Dorothy died, they had started to really get to know each other—bridging their thirteen-year age difference—having long talks while Tonia was at dance class down the road from his home. They would sit and drink coffee and talk about life. She opened up to him about some of the weight on her shoulders.

PEGGY REQUESTED THE FOLLOWING statement be included:

When I hear people complain about getting old, I think about how my sister would have done anything to have been able to grow old and watch her three children become adults and have children of their own.

It still feels like a nightmare that plays over and over again in your head. You just never get to wake up from it.

I still question did the police investigate her murder the way they would have had it been their sister, mother, child or wife? I have my doubts. You might ask me why they didn't even question my brother [Bob], *who had spent a considerable amount of time talking with Dotty on the Thursday before she was murdered. He called the* [Lewiston] *police station twice, as he felt he had some relevant information to tell them. They simply told him someone would get back to him. They never did! Why? In my mind it seems as though they didn't follow up on things they should have or maybe they were too focused on someone they thought my have committed this, or maybe they were covering up something or were they too busy to make sure no stone was left unturned.*

People think it must be very painful to talk or hear about her. The pain is not having her here with us! The pain is wondering if anyone cares enough about her to try and get justice for her.

I am happy and appreciate a book being written to tell the story of Dotty's life. I want to be able to read about her and to have others read about her life. I want people to get a glimpse of this beautiful person. I don't want the memory of her to die!

Short of someone confessing, I wish the cold case unit would devote the necessary time and resources to solving this case. I know there are other cases, but we have been waiting for almost fifty years to have some kind of resolution.

THE BEST FRIENDS

In her senior high school yearbook, Dorothy wrote:

These girls have really made my years in High the best years of my life. I will never forget one of them. And no person will ever be able to say anything bad about them to me. I won't take it. They really are the greatest girls I have ever met.

The last time Dorothy's friends saw her was mid- to late September 1976 at her house. The old gang from high school was all in town and wanted to see Dorothy and meet baby Peter. Sheila remembers everyone joking and laughing. Glenda remembers her friend being quieter than normal. When she asked Dorothy if she was afraid being on her own—when Peter would travel—in such a rural area, she dismissed the idea. That was very "Dorothy," Glenda and Diana say—she wasn't afraid of anything.

Sue recalls this scene from that night:

Tonia came in. She wanted to be a part of the group. She brought a newspaper clipping in and held it up for us to see. Dotty said, "Tonia honey, this is the night I've been waiting for, for so long. These are my best friends that I grew up with, and I really want to spend some time with them. Would you just play in the living room?" She said it so kind. "This night means so much to me to spend time with my friends." Tonia understood.

SHEILA'S HEART HURT FOR the brokenness of Dorothy's family. After her friend's murder, Glenda slept with a knife under her pillow. Sue remembers her friend's smile and how loyal she was. Diana says again and again how much she loved her.

MAINE COLD CASES

1970–1979

Mary C. Olenchuk

Thirteen-year-old Mary Olenchuk was last seen alive on August 9, 1970, near her family's summer home in Ogunquit, Maine, at approximately 5:00 p.m. An elderly resident of the Lookout Hotel saw her standing beside a maroon car, possibly a 1967 Chevy. The driver of the car was described as a white male, mid-thirties, wearing dark clothes. Olenchuk was 5'3", weighed eighty pounds and had dark-red shoulder-length hair.

The bicycle she had been riding was discovered around 11:00 p.m. in an archway of a local hotel.

Thirteen days later, Kennebunk patrolman George G. LeBarge and Peter Gunn, the caretaker for an estate near Parson's Beach in Kennebunk, Maine, found her badly decomposed body under two feet of loose hay in an abandoned barn in a heavily wooded area several miles from her home. At that time, some of the roads in the area were used as "lovers' lanes," while some were locked with heavy chains and padlocks. Police theorized death by strangulation.

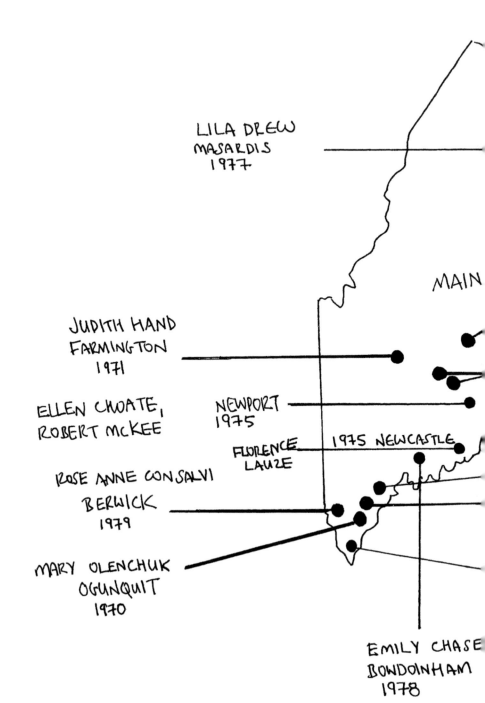

LILA DREW
MASARDIS
1977

MAIN

JUDITH HAND
FARMINGTON
1971

ELLEN CHOATE,
ROBERT MCKEE

NEWPORT
1975

FLORENCE
LAUZE

1975 NEWCASTLE

ROSE ANNE CONSALVI
BERWICK
1979

MARY OLENCHUK
OGUNQUIT
1970

EMILY CHASE
BOWDOINHAM
1978

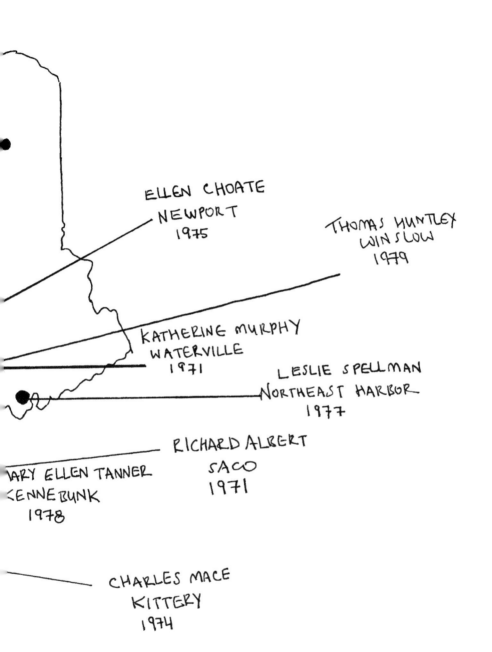

Hand-drawn map of unsolved homicides of females in Maine during the 1970s. *Map by author.*

Richard Albert

Bernard F. Underwood, twenty-seven, of Lowell, Massachusetts, escaped from the New Hampshire State Prison on August 26, 1971, by going over the wall by means of steel piping pieced together with small T-joints. He was serving a ten-to-fifteen-year sentence for assault and armed robbery.

Nearly three months later, on Thanksgiving Day, November 25, 1971, Richard Albert, thirty-two, of Dover, New Hampshire, and Robert Meuse, forty-four, of Chelsea, Massachusetts (*in some articles he is listed as being thirty-three years of age and from Hollywood, California), escaped from the same penitentiary by sawing through window bars in the prison bakery where they'd been working.

Albert was being held for federal authorities on charges including interstate transportation of a stolen motor vehicle. Meuse was serving a ten-to-twenty-year sentence for armed robbery.

On November 29, 1971, Underwood and Meuse held up the Southgate branch of the Nashua Trust Co. in Nashua, Massachusetts. They left with $2,500.

Meuse was disarmed during an assault on the twenty-seven-year-old manager of the Casco Bank & Trust Co. branch in Bridgton who was also an ex–Colby College football player.

Albert was found dead from a single gunshot wound in the head in a wooded area near the Maine Turnpike in Saco in April 1972. The body was believed to have been there for several months.

Underwood was recaptured on May 10, 1972.

Judith Hand

Blonde-haired, blue-eyed Judith Hand was reported missing at 8:15 p.m. on September 10, 1971, in Farmington, Maine. She returned home from school, where she had just started ninth grade, at 2:10 p.m. and approximately forty minutes later went to a neighbor's to collect babysitting money. It is believed she was taking a frequently used shortcut when something happened.

Her decomposing body was discovered thirteen days later by fifty-six-year-old Farmington officer Harold Hemingway under a sawdust pile at the site of a former mill, located at the end of Lincoln Street. The site, less than a mile from Hand's home and not over one hundred yards from a fraternity house at the University of Maine–Farmington was hidden from view by dense growth.

An intense search of the area had already been done. This was a follow-up search led by wardens of the Island Fisheries and Game Department, Farmington police and Franklin County sheriffs.

The autopsy failed to disclose the exact cause of death.

Prior to becoming a homicide detective, state police officer Lyndon Abbott worked on this case and got the impression people in the area knew more than they were saying during a neighborhood canvas.

It is believed state police know who killed her but have been unable to prove it.

Katherine Murphy

*This case is open, but inactive

On November 3, 1971, eighteen-year-old Colby College freshman Katherine Murphy was found fully clothed in a grassy ravine near the northeast edge of campus next to Mayflower Hill Drive. Initially, the theory was this was a hit-and-run fatality, not a homicide, thus Waterville police did not secure the area. By the time it was declared a homicide and the state police were brought in around twenty-four hours later, the scene had been trampled and evidence contaminated. It is believed she died as a result of multiple skull fractures caused by a blow by large blunt instrument.

Abbott worked on this case. He interviewed co-eds and found out Mayflower Hill Drive, where Murphy was found, was heavily traveled by students hitchhiking into Waterville. There was a corner off of the road in town locals called Colby Corner. That was where students would wait to get a ride back up to campus.

Alan Pelletier voluntarily gave police a statement that he was driving his pickup truck and saw a man beating a woman. He turned around, and the man was gone and Murphy's body face-down in the grass. From that point on, he was considered the prime suspect, with the theory being he accidentally hit her, she went down over the bank, he saw she was seriously injured but alive and killed hit her with a rock.

Unfortunately, the Waterville police released Pelletier's truck to his family. From there it disappeared; it was rumored the family crushed it or it was taken to a garage and repaired.

Abbott found out Pelletier used to brag about hauling girls from Colby up and back to the school. He was a very aggressive womanizer, and when he drank, he usually got drunk and was always looking to get laid. And he went after Colby girls.

In March 1986, Pelletier was indicted. His primary defense was that he had taken two polygraph tests and passed both of them. In January 1987, a Superior Court jury found Pelletier not guilty of the murder.

In 1999, during Albert Cochran's trial for murdering Janet Baxter, his attorney argued the shadow defendant's theory that Cochran was not responsible for Janet's murder but that other men were. He named several men around the same age and of the same group in the area: Perley Doyon, Armand Boudreau, Galen Lessard and Alan Pelletier. Nothing came of the claim, and Cochran was found guilty. *This case was removed from the Maine Unsolved Homicide site but is still open.

Later, state detective Dale Ames told Abbott he believed Pelletier had his buddy Armand Boudreau with him in the truck. Abbott says that's pure hearsay.

Charles Mace

In late September 1974, the nude decomposed body of nineteen-year-old Charles J. Mace was found by two hunters in an overgrown field about 125 feet from the Betty Welch Road in Kittery. Mace was wearing a gold ring with a green stone. He'd been shot. Mace had been missing from his home at 720 State Street in Portsmouth, New Hampshire, since late July 1974.

It's unconfirmed whether this is the same Charles Mace of 9 Prospect Street Portsmouth, New Hampshire, who was charged with conspiracy to sell a controlled drug on March 22, 1974.

Joyce Tanerillo

For details, see "The Unsolved Homicide Unit" chapter, page 130.

Ellen Choate

On June 26, 1977, the skeleton of Ellen Choate was found in a culvert hidden behind some brush off the Old County Road in Newport, Maine. She had been shot in the head.

The twenty-three-year-old was last seen on June 1, 1975, when she took a plane from Philadelphia, Pennsylvania, to Boston, Massachusetts, where authorities believe she either had a ride or was going to hitch to Newport to meet a friend or nearby Bangor for a teaching position. She'd been carrying a backpack and bedroll, was about 5'7" and 135 pounds with hazel eyes and light brown hair.

Several residents thought she lived in the Newport-Pittsfield area for about four years and was the daughter of a former Maine Central Institute teacher in Pittsfield who was also a Newport minister.

There is a possibility her death is connected with the slaying of Robert McKee, thirty-five, a teacher of the sixth grade at the Vickery School in Pittsfield, who had been moonlighting at a Texaco station in Newport when shot three times during an unwitnessed robbery on June 20, 1975.

Florence E. Lauze

On August 16, 1975, the partially clothed body of nineteen-years-old Florence E. (Norcross) Lauze of 565 East Street Brockton, Massachusetts, was found floating in Sherman Lake in Newcastle, Maine. According to the August 21, 1975 edition of *The Lincoln County News*, she was "wearing a long-sleeve dark blue jersey top, underwear, blue socks, low brown shoes with crepe soles and several pieces of jewelry."

Initially, the incident was reported as a drowning. However, it turned out she'd been strangled. Her father was a resident of Damariscotta, Maine. It's possible she was hitchhiking and that she was unemployed at the time of her death. Previously, she was employed as a nurse's aide at St. Joseph's Manor Nursing Home in Brockton, Massachusetts. Attempts to track down more information on Lauze from both the nursing home and the owners of the home—the Sisters of Jesus Crucified, Our Lady of Sorrows Convent—proved futile. Staff were very helpful but have no written records from that time.

Robert McKee

In June 1975, Robert McKee, a thirty-five-year-old elementary schoolteacher and father of two young children, was shot to death between midnight and 4:00 a.m. during a robbery while moonlighting at his summer job as an attendant at McNally's Texaco station in Newport, Maine. He was working alone. Between $400 and $600 was taken.

Dale Ames was lead investigator, with Lyndon Abbott assisting. According to Abbott, it became apparent McKee was not supposed to be working that night. He was subbing for someone else.

Ames and Abbott believe, but have no evidence to prove the theory, that when the robbers came in, they expected to see the other guy who was supposed to be working. They recognized McKee and he them, and they shot him. Ames and Abbott don't think the perpetrators planned the murder.

Lila Drew

In the late afternoon on March 18, 1977, the battered body of seventy-eight-year-old Lila Drew was found in her home in the tiny rural town of Masardis in Northern Maine. The widow and retired schoolteacher may have been dead for about twenty-four hours.

Dale Ames was lead investigator, with Lyndon Abbott assisting on this case.

Abbott found a male relative of Drew's had tried to get money from his grandmother, but she would give him only a little. The night of the murder, the young man went over to an older gentleman's house—a guy he drank with—and borrowed a snowmobile from him for a couple of hours the night Drew was murdered. Police found snow mobile tracks around her home. According to Abbott, local folks said the young man was seen buying drinks and waving money around.

Ames and Abbott believe this person killed Drew but were unable to prove it. Abbott says another state police officer investigated the individual, who spent time in Presque Isle, a larger town about thirty miles from Masardis.

Leslie Spellman

The partly clad body of twenty-six-year-old Leslie Spellman of Hingham, Massachusetts was found in the Asticou Azalea Gardens in Northeast

Harbor, Maine, around 9:30 a.m. on June 19, 1977. She'd been bludgeoned to death but not sexually assaulted. Her dog was located alive a mile from the manicured gardens of the popular Asticou Inn.

She was last seen alive on June 18 in Barre, Vermont, by her younger sister Amy. The two had backpacked around the state before Amy headed home, and Leslie said she was hitching to Acadia National Park.

Emily Chase

On Saturday, January 21, 1978, Emily Chase of Center Street in Bowdoinham celebrated her ninetieth birthday with family. The group ate birthday cake, presented Mrs. Chase with a television and reminisced about her time married to lighthouse keeper Captain Almon Mitchell and how the couple lived on Ram Island in Boothbay Harbor for thirteen years.

At 9:30 a.m. on February 19, Mrs. Chase's battered body was found in her home. It is believed she was beaten to death the night before.

Mrs. Chase had seven children, forty-three grandchildren and ninety-four great-grandchildren.

Detective Bruce Rafnell, who had Dorothy's case, coordinated the investigation.

Mary Ellen Tanner

A few weeks after she turned eighteen and two months before she began her senior year at Kennebunk High School, Mary Ellen Tanner's life ended.

On the evening of July 7, 1978, she attended parties in a wooded section of Route 9 in Kennebunk and at the Kennebunk Beach. Tanner left the Kennebunk Beach gathering in the company of friends and was dropped off at the intersection of Routes 9 and 35 in Kennebunk at approximately 11:30 p.m. after she indicated she was going to hitchhike home. Two days later, her body was discovered in Gracie Evans Airfield in Lyman about thirty miles away.

According to her autopsy, Tanner had multiple head lacerations and blunt injuries to the body and neck. She was also found to be three months pregnant.

Tanner had been active on the gymnastics team, in the school's glee club and with the majorettes. She was employed for the summer at the Glen-Mor Restaurant in Kennebunk.

Rose Anne Consavli
(also known as Rose Anne Fitzpatrick)

The body of twenty-four-year-old Rose Anne from Malden, Massachusetts, was found on a wooded road off Route 9 in Berwick, Maine, on July 25, 1979, at 1:25 p.m. An autopsy showed she died from multiple stab wounds to the neck and body the night before. Her street address was listed as 51 Lisbon Street.

She was an exotic dancer. It's possible she was associated with a motorcycle club based in Massachusetts.

Thomas Huntley

Thomas Huntley, who has been described in his early thirties, died in a house fire on April 12, 1979. An employee of the Scott Paper Co.'s Hinckley plant, he lived in a one-family wooden home on Route 137 in Winslow, Maine, with his wife and two daughters. Huntley's wife was out shopping with one of their two daughters the morning of the fire and arrived home shortly after firemen discovered the body.

It is believed he was asleep when the fire started, woke up and tried to escape but was overcome by smoke by the time he reached the living room.

Initially, the fire, which began midmorning, was attributed to an electrical malfunction. By late June, authorities believed otherwise and were continuing to investigate further. By September, authorities had concluded it was arson and were treating Huntley's death as a suspicious one.

IF YOU HAVE ANY information about any of these cases, please contact: Maine State Police, Major Crimes Unit-Central, 36 Hospital Street | Augusta, ME, 04330 | (207) 624-7076 x9.

SOURCES

1. Forever Young

Hometown

Digital Maine Repository. "Population 1960 and 1966." https://digitalmaine.com.

Maine, an Encyclopedia. "Sabattus." https://maineanencyclopedia.com.

Family

Lewiston Sun Journal. "Featherweight Maurice 'Lefty' Lachance Added Punch to Lewiston's Boxing History." August 21, 2022.

Patric and Stokes, Cdr Edward. *Destroyer Life: The USS George E. Badger in World War II*. Self-published, 1994.

Wikipedia. "SS George E. Badger" https://en.wikipedia.org.

———. "William Brewster" https://en.wikipedia.org.

Best Friends

Bill Maroldo's Facebook page

NavSource Online. "USS William H. Standley." Cruiser Photo Archive. http://www.navsource.org.

YouTube. "Royal Knights—Pal Hop Days." www.youtube.com.

The Woman

Lewiston Daily Sun. "Motorists Appear in 9th District Court." July 11, 1967.

————. Police beat. October 21, 1967.

Lewiston Evening Journal. Divorce announcement/court listing. June 1, 1971.

Lewiston Sun Journal. Gerald Arsenault obituary. November 7, 2008.

National Park Service. "WAVES." https://www.nps.gov.

Portland Evening Express. "Wyo. Youth Killed by Car on Naples Road." July 1, 1967.

Portland Press Herald. "Lisbon Youth Fined in Highway Death." July 7, 1967.

The Night

Cook, Kevin. *Kitty Genovese: The Murder, the Bystanders, the Crime that Changed America*. W.W. Norton & Company, 2014.

Gansberg, Martin. "Kew Gardens Slaying: A Look Back." *New York Times*, March 17, 1974.

————. "37 Who Saw Murder Didn't Call the Police; Apathy at Stabbing of Queens Woman Shocks Inspector." *New York Times*, March 27, 1964.

Haberman, Clyde. "Remembering Kitty Genovese." *New York Times*, April 10, 2016.

Oblinger, Jan. "Body Discovered at Laundromat." *Lewiston Evening Journal*, November 6, 1976.

Weather Underground. Augusta, ME, weather forecast November 6, 1976. https://www.wunderground.com.

2. A Murder Investigation

Morning Watch

Bangor Daily News. "Troopers to Take Course." January 27, 1976.

Beegan, Daniel. "Homicides in Maine not high." Associated Press, December 14, 1976.

Beeline Fashions Facebook public group, former Beeline employees and field salespeople.

Day, John S. "Slayings in State Growing More Impersonal." *Bangor Daily News,* December 14, 1976.

Disaster Center. Maine Crime Rates (data in the crime reports is derived from the annual Uniform Crime Reports issued by the FBI) 1960–2019. https://www.disastercenter.com.

Footman, Coonie. "AG's Office Continues Probe into Apparent Lisbon Falls Homicide." *Lewiston Evening Journal,* April 5, 1976.

Grape, Nancy. "Body Is Found in Horse Barn." *Lewiston Evening Journal,* November 6, 1976.

Kennebec Journal. Obituary Willard F. Parker. November 13, 1993.

Lewiston Daily Sun. Murder notice Shirley Baldwin. April 5, 1976.

Lewiston Evening Journal. Watch assignments. August 30, 1976.

Lewiston Sun Journal. Obituary of Roger A. Bisson. November 14, 2010.

Mills, Janet. Eulogy of Dr. Henry F. Ryan. May 26, 2017.

Oblinger, Jan. "Body Discovered at Laundromat." *Lewiston Evening Journal,* November 6, 1976.

Quinlan, Elaine. "Liberty Residents Frightened After Double Slaying There." *Morning Sentinel,* December 15, 1973.

Sanford Tribune. "MSP Notes Surge in Homicides." December 20, 1976.

Making Notifications

Lewiston Evening Journal. "Trooper Lionel Cote Named Sabattus Chief." July 2, 1974.

The Day Shift

Carson, Michael. "Cohen to Discuss Slaying with LPD." *Lewiston Daily Sun*, November 10, 1976.

Grape, Nancy. "Body Is Found in Horse Barn." *Lewiston Evening Journal*. November 6, 1976.

Lewiston Sun Journal. "Lewiston Police Effort In Homicides Is Lauded." November 8, 1976.

The Postmortem

Dehner, Louis P., MD. "The Medical Autopsy: Past, Present, and Dubious Future." *Journal of the Missouri State Medical Association* 107, no. 2 (March–April 2010): 94–100.

Mills, Janet. Eulogy of Dr. Henry F. Ryan. May 26, 2017.

Office of the Maine Attorney General. www.maine.gov.

Plumer, Mary. "Ryan Hopes for Morgue in Second Term." *Kennebec Journal*, July 16, 1983.

The Other Murders

Bangor Daily News. "Jury Finds Man Guilty of Stables Slaying." April 4, 1977.

Grape, Nancy. "Body Is Found in Horse Barn." *Lewiston Evening Journal*, November 6, 1976.

Lewiston Daily Sun. "North Jay Woman Arraigned." November 10, 1976.

Lewiston Evening Journal. "Accused McBride Slayer Is Arraigned Today." November 8, 1976.

Oblinger, Jan. "Body Discovered at Laundromat." *Lewiston Evening Journal*, November 6, 1976.

Times Record. "Suspect Is Charged in Beating Death." November 8, 1976.

Stakeout and Antique Theft Ring

Bangor Daily News. "Regional Antiques Stole Items Under Contract." August 8, 1979.

Journal Tribune. "Pair Found Guilty in Home Invasion." August 13, 1994.

Kennebec Journal. "Livermore Falls Man Gets 30 Years for Home Invasion." November 19, 1994.

———. "Men Face Hearing in Home Invasion." April 12, 1994.

LaFlamme, Mark. "Who Killed Dorothy." *Sun Journal,* February 19, 2001.

Lewiston Daily Sun. Arrest listings Lionel Lussier, Michael Boucher. October 16, 1976.

———. Eighth District Court listings. December 2, 1972.

———. "Lisbon Men Appeal Jail Terms in Grenham Assault." March 20, 1973.

———. "State Rests in Boucher Assault Case." December 21, 1976.

———. "Tussle with Motorcycle Club Gets Man Four Months in Jail." December 6, 1985.

Lewiston Sun Journal. "Cited for Contempt, Gets 10 Days." May 13, 1971.

———. "Detectives Find Stolen Antiques." August 29, 1979.

———. "More Indictments Expected in Antique Ring Probe." May 5, 1978.

———. "Officer Is 'Satisfactory' After Nightclub Scuffle." February 10, 1973.

———. "Two Sentenced by Violette." January 23, 1974.

Manlove, George. "Lisbon Falls Man Acquitted of Assault in Superior Court." *Lewiston Daily Sun,* November 6, 1985.

Morning Sentinel. "21st Antique-Theft Conviction." May 3, 1979.

Sullivan, Jennifer. "Fourth Man Indicted in Litchfield Incident." *Sun Journal,* April 7, 1994.

Times Record. "Topsham House Has Sensitive Alarm." June 2, 1976

Veeder, Katrina. "Last Man Sentenced in Home Invasion." *Bangor Daily News.* December 17, 1994.

Wilson, Catherine. "Four Area Men Arrested for Theft of Antiques." *Times Record,* August 1, 1978.

Welcome to Lewiston

Berube, Gerald P. Annual Report Lewiston, Maine.

Carson, Michael. "Commissioner Aliberti Charges Mismanagement in Police Dept." *Lewiston Daily Sun,* February 24, 1977.

Deveau, Sharon. "If He Needs the Police, He Knows They'll Be Good." *Lewiston Journal,* February 29, 1980.

Herrling, Mac. "My First Job: Summer Cop in Lewiston in 1972." Bates College. https://www.bates.edu.

Leamon, James S. *"Historic Lewiston: A Textile City in Transition."* Lewiston Historical Commission, 1976. www.lewistonmaine.gov.

Lewis Daily Sun. "Younger Longtin Injured While Cleaning Shotgun." December 20, 1976.

Lewiston Evening Journal. "As We See It: Policy Change Needed." December 20, 1976.

Robustelli, Tom. "AVRPC Asks Grant to Establish Crime Task Force." *Sun Journal*, February 1, 1980.

Sun Journal. "Sweeping Changes Made in PD." May 8, 1968.

Taylor, Scott. "On Lisbon Street, Social Clubs and Taverns' Heyday Long Gone." *Sun Journal*, August 29, 2010.

U.S. Census Bureau. "Number of Inhabitants Maine." www2.census.gov.

It's Always the Husband

Bangor Daily News. Arrest log Presque Isle. May 25, 1973.

Lewiston Daily Sun. Arrest log. August 29, 1970.

———. Arrest log. October 1, 1970.

———. "Book Lisbon Man On Driving Charge." July 19, 1969.

———. "Trio Apprehended at Lisbon Falls." October 28, 1967.

———. "Youths Booked on Liquor Violations." February 10, 1968.

Sun Journal. Arrest log. October 1, 1969.

———. Arrest log. September 29, 1971.

Another Woman

Bangor Daily News. "Cochran Case a DNA Bellwether." May 29, 1999.

Belleville News-Democrat. "Slayer of 4 Gets 50–75 Year Term." September 30, 1964.

Calder, Amy. "After Convicted Killer Dies, Police Plead for Help Finding Clues in Central Maine Woman's Death." Central Maine. www.centralmaine.com.

Chicago Tribune. "Accused Wife Killer Admits Guilt at Trial." September 30, 1964.

———. "Father Tells Why He Killed His Children." February 19, 1964.

Hertz, Bruce. "40 Quizzed in Murder." *Bangor Daily News*, November 26, 1976.

Lizotte, Thomas. "Oakland Woman Is Murdered." *Central Maine Morning Sentinel*, November 25, 1976.

———. "State Police Comb Area for Baxter-Killing Clues." *Central Maine Morning Sentinel*, November 27, 1976.

———. "State Police Seek To Pinpoint Slain Woman's Moves." *Central Maine Morning Sentinel*, November 29, 1976.

Morning Sentinel. "Sophisticated Forensic Science Used in 21-Year-Old Murder." March 18, 1998.

The Times. "Murder Trial of Joliet Man Opens Today." September 14, 1964.

Growing Cold

Carson, Michael. "Beaten to Death: Authorities Pressing Woman's Slaying Probe." *Lewiston Daily Sun*, November 9, 1976.

———. "Cohen Claims No New Leads in Milliken Murder Investigation." *Lewiston Daily Sun*, February 3, 1977.

Grape, Nancy. "A Lewiston Killer Still Not Caught." *Lewiston Evening Journal*, November 7, 1977.

Lewiston Daily Sun. "Cohen to Set Meeting Friday." November 12, 1976.

———. "LPD Intensifying Search for Milliken Murderer." December 8, 1976.

Lewiston Evening Journal. "No Holiday for Murder Probers." November 10, 1976.

———. "Two More Are Investigating Woman's Death." December 8, 1976.

Morning Sentinel. "1976 Lewiston Murder Haunts Victim's Family." March 22, 1994.

Sun Journal. "More Information Supplied Police Investigating the Milliken Murder." February 22, 1979.

———. "No Let-Up in Probe of Death." November 12, 1976.

———. Obituary Robert Soucy. September 30, 2022.

Times Record. "Lead in Murder." October 3, 1978.

3. Unsolved

The Original Detective

Hongoltz-Hetling, Matt. "After 50 Years, Story of Benton Ghost Resurrected." Central Maine. October 27, 2013. www.centralmaine.com.

Kennebec Journal. "7 State Troopers Promoted." August 23, 1979.

State v. Stackpole. JUSTIA US Law. December 12, 1975. https://law.justia. com.

Thayer, Brian. "Girl's Death Laid to Strangulation, Exposure." *Bangor Daily News*, February 2, 1972.

Wikipedia. "Frances Glessner Lee." https://en.wikipedia.org.

The Unsolved Homicide Unit

Associated Press. "Cherryfield Man's Death Probed." March 1, 1983.

———. "Girl Chum Saw Missing Boy in Auto." July 27, 1954.

———. "No Trace of Missing Youth." July 26, 1954.

———. "Wood Boy Murdered by Sex Fiend; Body Discovered in River." August 1, 1954.

Campbell, Steve. "South Portland Woman's Strangulation Death Remains Mystery." *Evening Express*, December 11, 1989.

Department of Public Safety, Maine State Police. "Unsolved Homicides." https://www.maine.gov.

As of September 21, 2024, the Maine State Police Unsolved Homicide webpage states:

According to her husband, Tanerillo was last seen alive at 0100 hours on 8/26/1974 by her ex-husband whom she agreed to have coffee and talk with. After talking, she left, picked up a hitchhiker on Congress Street in Portland, then ran three red lights. Her ex-husband stated that he followed her and lost her at the lights.

*When asked for a comment regarding why the Maine State Police account is different from that of the husband's reported in the press, Lieutenant Pickering declined. However, it's possible the Maine State Police has information that has not been released.

Dirigo Safety. Michael Chavez instructor biography. https://dirigosafety.com.

Dougherty, Patty. "Woman's Death Investigated." *Bangor Daily News*, August 28, 1984.

Ellsworth American. "The Kramer Case." February 28, 1985.

Evening Express. "Gunshots Caused Death." *Evening Express*, March 2, 1983.

———. "Police Await Answer in Tanerillo Death." August 27, 1974.

———. "Police Press Investigation into Divorcee's Murder." August 30, 1974.

———. "Search Continues For Boy, 12, Missing From So. Gray Home." July 24, 1954.

Facebook. "Sean Conway Cold Case." https://www.facebook.com.

Find a Grave. "Daniel Kenneth Wood Jr." www.findagrave.com.

Harlow, Doug. "Madison Man Slain." *Morning Sentinel*, April 7, 1994.

———. "Madison Shooting Remains Unsolved." *Morning Sentinel*, April 11, 1994.

———. "State Police Still Need Help." *Morning Sentinel*, April 23, 1994.

Heidinger, Katherine. "Hunt On for 'More than One' in Slaying of Police Tipster." *Ellsworth American*, March 3, 1983.

———. "Six Men Still Assigned to Kramer Death Probe." *Ellsworth American*, April 14, 1983.

Hench, David. "Clue Surfaces in Boy's 1954 Murder." *Portland Press Herald*, April 7, 2003.

Holmes, Ken. "Murder in Maine." *Kennebec Journal*, July 5, 1978.

Journal Tribune. "Investigators Look for Help in Murder Case." January 29, 1991.

———. "Woman's Skeleton Is Identified." November 23, 1982.

Kisonak, Richard. "Hunt Sex Fiend in Slaying of Danny Wood, 12." *Lewiston Daily Sun*, August 2, 1954.

———. "State Offers $1,000 Reward in Wood Case." *Lewiston Daily Sun*, August 5, 1954.

Mack, Sharon. "Police Appeal to Public in Investigation of Madison Slaying." *Bangor Daily News*, April 9, 1994.

Portland Press Herald. Obituary Sebato Anthony Tanerillo "Sonny." April 19, 2020.

———. "Police Seek Gray Youth Missing Since Thursday." July 24, 1954.

Seavey, Kristen. "The Maine Cold Case of Raynald Levesque." *Murder She Told*. March 30, 2022. https://www.murodershetold.com.

Sturler, Alice De. "Daniel K. Wood Jr." Defrosting Cold Cases. November 20, 2017. https://defrostingcoldcases.com.

Sun Journal. "Foul Play Suspected in S. Portland Death." August 27, 1974.

Times Record. "Cherryfield Man's Death Probed." *Times Record*, March 1, 1983.

———. "Police Investigate Death." August 29, 1974.

The Forensics

University of Leicester. "DNA Fingerprinting." https://le.ac.uk.
Wikipedia. "Locard's Exchange Principle." https://en.wikipedia.org.
————. "Paul Kirk." https://en.wikipedia.org.

4. The Unknown

The Theories

Bangor Daily News. "Blunt Weapon Killed Debra Dill." September 17, 1973.
Biddeford-Saco Journal. "Battered Body Is Found Sunday." September 17, 1973.
Daily Kennebec Journal. "In Memoriam Debra Dill." September 16, 1974.
————. "Kenneth Gilman Appointed to Hallowell Police Force." December 14, 1972.
————. "Officer Is Certified Aid Man." *Daily Kennebec Journal*, March 2, 1973.
Farkas, Tom. "Boucher Sentenced to Life in Dill Murder." *Morning Sentinel*, July 17, 1991.
————. "Judge Says No New Trial for Murderer of Debra Dill." *Kennebec Journal*, September 4, 1991.
————. "Witnesses Link Boucher with Dill Case." *Kennebec Journal*, July 11, 1991.
LaFlamme, Mark. "Who Killed Dorothy." *Sun Journal*, February 19, 2001.
Lewiston Daily Sun. "Academy to Graduate Area Officers." December 20, 1973.
————. "Police Officers Go to Academy." November 7, 1973.
————. "Two Officers Hired, but No Detective Appointed." June 27, 1973.
Lewiston Evening Journal. "New Police Dept. Members Begin Duties Today." July 2, 1973.
————. "Police Personalities: Officer Gilman." August 10, 1974.
McCrary, Gregg O. *The Unknown Darkness: Profiling the Predators Among Us*. HarperTorch, 2004.

Another Version of the Story

Bangor Daily News. "Jury Finds Man Guilty of Stables Slaying." April 4, 1977.
Evening Express. "Suspect Faces Court in 1 of 3 Killings." November 8, 1976.

Hodgman, Cliff. "Judge Oks Use of Snow's Statements." *Lewiston Evening Journal*, April 1, 1977.

JUSTIA US Law. Supreme Judicial Court of Maine—State v. Snow. April 5, 1978. https://law.justia.com.

Kennebec Journal. "Night of Slaying Described." April 2, 1977.

Lewiston Daily Sun. Clemency Notice State of Maine. November 4, 1985.

Oblinger, Jan. "Snow Enters No Plea; Hearing Slated Nov. 22." *Lewiston Evening Journal*, November 8, 1976.

———."Witness at Snow Probable Cause Hearing Won't Answer Questions." *Lewiston Evening Journal*, November 22, 1976.

Reed, Gerald. "Scott Snow Is Indicted on First Degree Homicide Count." *Lewiston Daily Sun*, December 14, 1976.

Times Record. "Suspect Is Charged in Beating Death." November 8, 1976.

5. *The Survivors*

The Daughters

Cain, Stephanie. "Milliken Case Won't Be Aired by TV Show." *Sun Journal*, October 25, 1995.

———. "Police Review Milliken Murder Case." *Sun Journal*, October 21, 1995.

———. "Woman Wants Mother's 1976 Murder Solved." *Sun Journal*, July 29, 1995.

Central Maine Morning. "1976 Lewiston Murder Haunts Victim's Family." March 22, 1994.

Sunday Sun Journal. "Open Slaying Prompts Reward." November 5, 2006.

WGME. "Daughter of Murdered Mother Still Seeking Answers 45 Years Later." November 6, 2021.

WMTW. "Maine Woman Seeks Justice 45 Years after Mother Killed." November 5, 2021.

Maine Cold Cases: 1970–1979

Bangor Daily News. "Body Is Identified." September 29, 1974.

———. "Motorists' Aid Sought in Slaying." June 24, 1975.

————. "Police Can't Verify Report of Slaying." July 31, 1979.

Boston Globe. "Funeral Rites Tomorrow for Slain Brockton Woman." August 28, 1975.

Brown, Jeannette. "On Floor of Service Station." *Morning Sentinel*, June 21, 1975.

————. "People Made the News in Newport During '75." *Morning Sentinel*, December 31, 1975.

Buckley, Ken. "Search on for Girl's Slayer." *Bangor Daily News*, August 24, 1970.

Charles, Richard W. "Girl Search Intense but So Far Futile." *Portland Press Herald*, August 16, 1970.

Colby Echo. "Kathy Murphy." November 4, 1971. https://digitalcommons.colby.edu.

Concord Monitor. "Escapee Sighting 'Mistaken Identity.'" November 29, 1971.

Dauphinals, Wendy. "Pelletier Indictment Arouses Bad Memories of Student's Murder." *Colby Echo*, March 20, 1986. https://digitalcommons.colby.edu.

Department of Public Safety, Maine State Police. "Unsolved Homicides." https://www.maine.gov.

Ellsworth American. "Eight Years Later Leslie Spellman Murder Case Still Under Investigation." June 20, 1985.

————. "Murder Investigation Turns to Vermont." June 30, 1977.

Emmons, Lee. "Forty-Five Years On, a Newcastle Murder Remains Unsolved." *Lincoln County News*, August 16, 2020.

Evening Express. "Body of Man Shot to Death Is Identified." September 28, 1974.

————. "Pike Body That of N.H. Escapee." April 21, 1972.

Harrison, Fran. "Fatigue, Frustration Daily Companions of Police Detectives." *Journal Tribune*, July 27, 1978.

Higgins, Jill. "Police Check New Lead in 1978 Slaying." *Portland Press Herald*, August 12, 1996.

Kennebec Journal. "Strangled Woman Identified." August 27, 1975.

Lewiston Daily Sun. "Body Found at Kittery Identified." September 28, 1974.

————. "Maine Gas Stations Organize Reward Fund Against Holdups." August 26, 1975.

Morning Sentinel. "Farmington Girl Reported Missing." September 13, 1971.

————. "Former Colby Man Captures Escaped Convict." December 14, 1971.

————. "General's Daughter Believed Abducted." August 12, 1970.

————. "Slain Woman's Body Identified." July 28, 1979.

————. "2 Escape from Prison in N.H." November 26, 1971.

Nemitz, Bill. "April Winslow Fire Probed." *Morning Sentinel*, June 30, 1979.

————. "Pelletier Indicted in 1971 Murder." *Morning Sentinel*, March 8, 1986.

————. "Winslow Man Dies in House Fire." *Morning Sentinel*, April 13, 1979.

Noonan, Melinda, and Sara Smith. "Woman's Death Investigated as Homicide." *Journal Tribune*, July 10, 1978.

Norris, Floyd. "Loaded Revolver Found in State Prison Cell." *Concord Monitor*, November 16, 1972.

Portland Press Herald. "Victim's Dad—News Missed the Real Mary." August 14, 1996.

Portsmouth Herald. "Grand Jury." June 15, 1974.

————. "Granite State: Two Prison Escapees Still Loose." November 29, 1971.

————. "U.S. Warrants." December 3, 1971.

Rankin, Joe. "Witness: Kelley Story Fiction." *Morning Sentinel*, May 20, 1999.

Rhodes, Dean. "Widow's Murder Leaves Masardis in State of Shock." *Bangor Daily News*, March 28, 1977.

Rosenthal, Larry. "Fatal Winslow Fire in April Ruled Arson." *Morning Sentinel*, September 5, 1979.

Seavey, Kristen. "Maine Unsolved: Mary Ellen Tanner, Parts One and Two." *Murder She Told*. July 5 and 6, 2023. https://www.murdershetold.com.

————. "The Unsolved Case of Judith Hand." *Murder She Told*. February 13, 2024. https://www.murdershetold.com.

Sun Journal. "Farmington Body Believed That of Missing Girl." September 23, 1971.

————. "Meuse Sentenced for Bank Robbery." November 7, 1972.

————. "Officials Make Tentative Identification of Body." September 24, 1971.

Times Record. "Celebrates 90th." January 27, 1978.

————. "Elderly Woman Slain in Bowdoinham Home." February 20, 1978.

————. "Man Dies in Fire." April 13, 1979.

Valley News. "Prisoner Found Dead." April 24, 1972.

Williams, Maureen. "Police Release Details About Slaying Victim." *Bangor Daily News*, June 24, 1977.

Interviews and Conversations

Mary Ellen A.
Lyndon Abbott
Karen and Dennis Atwood
Ronald Bourget Esq.
Joan Caron
Mike Chavez, Maine State Police
Ann and Mike Deslauriers
Diana F.
Charlie Frazer
Joseph L. Giacalon
Alison Gingras, Maine State
  Police Crime Laboratory
Don Goulet
Neal Goulet
Dr. Margaret Greenwald
Dave Gudas
Susan and Geoffrey H.
William Healy
Mac Herrling
Cynthia Homer, Maine State
  Police Crime Laboratory
Benjamin H.
Glenys K.
Susan Lauria

Mona Maillet
Bill Maroldo
Peter McCarthy
Jon Mennealy
Peter Milliken
Mark Nickerson, president of the
  Maine State Troopers
Sheila O.
Peggy and Moe P.
Reggie and Claire P.
Sue P.
Mike Parks
Lieutenant Thomas Pickering,
  Maine State Police
Bob Prince
George R.
Debbie Reitchel
Tonia Ross
Dr. Marcella Sorg
Jeff Taber
Percy Turner
Glenda W.
Gail Winchell